Making Mobiles

Bruce Cana Fox

4880 Lower Valley Road, Atglen, PA 19310 USA

Front Cover:
(top left) "Ambiguous Two" mobile by Bruce Cana Fox
(center) "White Cascade" mobile by Bruce Cana Fox
(bottom right) "Two Red" mobile by Bruce Cana Fox

Title Page: "Transit of Venus" mobile by Bruce Cana Fox

Other Schiffer Books on Related Subjects:
George Rickey, The Early Years Maxwell Davidson III
The World of Bertoia Nancy N. Schiffer and Val O. Bertoia

Copyright © 2006 by Bruce Cana Fox
Library of Congress Control Number: 2006926881

Designed by Mark David Bowyer
Type set in Geometric 231 Hv BT / Korinna BT

ISBN: 0-7643-2474-8
Printed in China

Published by Schiffer Publishing Ltd.
4880 Lower Valley Road
Atglen, PA 19310
Phone: (610) 593-1777; Fax: (610) 593-2002
E-mail: Info@schifferbooks.com

For the largest selection of fine reference books on this and related subjects, please visit our web site at
www.schifferbooks.com
We are always looking for people to write books on new and related subjects. If you have an idea for a book please contact us at the above address.

This book may be purchased from the publisher.
Include $3.95 for shipping.
Please try your bookstore first.
You may write for a free catalog.

In Europe, Schiffer books are distributed by
Bushwood Books
6 Marksbury Ave.
Kew Gardens
Surrey TW9 4JF England
Phone: 44 (0) 20 8392-8585; Fax: 44 (0) 20 8392-9876
E-mail: info@bushwoodbooks.co.uk
Website: www.bushwoodbooks.co.uk
Free postage in the U.K., Europe; air mail at cost.

Contents

1. Introduction 4

2. First Mobile— Lightweight Sample 6

3. Materials 17

4. Tool Selection 20

5. Mobile Design 28

6. Cutting Elements 29

7. Forming The Bail 34

8. Balancing the Horizontal Element 38

9. Horizontal Element Connection Rod 42

10. Vertical Element Connecting Rod 47

11. Rivet Removal and Other Repairs 53

12. Hanging and Swivels 56

13. Finishing Considerations 62

14. Painting 65

15. Reassembly and Final Tweaks 69

16. Packing and Hanging 72

17. Expanding On Basic Designs 75

18. Developing a Personal Style 77

19. Sources for Tools and Materials 79

Recommended Reading 80

Chapter 1

Introduction

Why bother with making mobiles at all? Inexpensive colorful stuff is available from many fine manufacturers that can be hung from the ceiling to provide visual stimulation. There are two types of mobiles produced by these manufacturers. In one type various bright bits are hung by threads from sticks or rods. A second type has vertically oriented elements balanced on wires attached to those elements.

This book instructs the reader in a third, more difficult, method involving horizontally balanced elements. I believe these constructions are more visually satisfying, especially when the observer is looking up at the mobile.

I propose here to enumerate several reasons, perhaps no one of them sufficient in and of itself, to carry one through the efforts of mobile construction, but if three or four of them are taken together, one may muster the motivation needed to carry the enterprise.

The first, and often the inner reason most compelling to start on a path of constructing difficult horizontal element mobiles is that of pure ego gratification. To stand before mortal friends and relatives, displaying such a marvelous creation, with the inner glow that comes from the realization that none of them could build what you have, results in no little self-satisfaction. It is hard to deny that we all have a bit of that within, and sometimes in unguarded moments we let others see it too. But, it seems not to get one very far down the path of life. Sometimes we can be brought up short by the realization that most of the admiring crowd can do something that the creator can not. It is then that other reasons are needed if one is to continue and progress.

It may be best to admit the ego element, make friends with it, and then go on to find more compelling reasons to keep up such difficult tasks.

When encountering an especially well done or creative art work, beginning artists often think, "Wow, I want to make one like THAT!" If you have stood under a mobile by Alexander Calder and entertained such thoughts, this book will help you "make one like that." Once again, this would not be reason enough to continue the process, but if ultimately the process is satisfying, why should we care what it took to get started?

There are meditative aspects to mobile construction. While I doubt my Zen roshi friend would put the repetitive tasks of filing the edges of mobile elements in the same category of strict zazen sitting meditation, even he would recognize the mentally relaxing aspects of this practice. One does get in a bit of a zone once the frustrations of handling the tools and materials are overcome. This all presupposes that you actually like the processes described herein. I propose that you try to build a mobile and see. If you have gotten this far in the introduction, chances are you liked the pictures and have the motivation to go on.

Why else? The work flow of conception, design, planning, producing parts, balancing the work, finishing it, and then displaying it has a satisfying organization to it. One can see progress all the way through the process. Once a little control of the medium has been acquired the sense of progress can be quite remarkable. And control over the aluminum and balance is control over a small part of our lives. This work flow can come to be a nice little cycle of life. We grasp at a desired shape, form, and motion. Then we grasp further to acquire materials, tools, and skills to realize the idea. Then we design and plan. Then there are the actual construction delights. Then we hang it, observe it, and finally give it away. Then we are free to start grasping all over again.

And we make the inanimate somewhat animate. The sheets and rods, wires and rivets become animated by gentle breezes.

Organization is created from a chaos of sheet metal trimmings, wire bits, and file dust amidst a clutter of tools.

Something special can be created to fit in a particular space.

Very special and individual gifts can be created, often resulting in a big "Ooooo" factor reward.

And of course, for many of us guy-shaped organisms, there is the excuse to buy more tools.

On the one hand we may ask why spend so much time on mere visual delights. On the other hand, what else were you doing with that time? Here is something to do that is way better than to veg out, hypno-snacking in front of the tube having corporate pabulum irradiating your memory cells thirty times a second. Each moment happens only once and you have opportunities to do something with that moment, or not. They tell you to get a massage, drink more water, take a vacation, get a hobby, change jobs, go back to school, get a new car, fix the old car, go for walks, attend a twelve step meeting, start a journal, ask for praise, give praise, buy flowers, cry, laugh, rage, feel the pain, move on. So add to all the sage advice another category, "make a mobile."

Will building mobiles change your life? Yes and no. Building mobiles can't bring the total change generated by a tsunami or hurricane sweeping all your relations and possessions out to sea. Building a mobile will change one moment, then another, then still other moments. The moments of planning, cutting metal, balancing shapes and colors are moments in which you are not doing something else. There will be changes with the choices of each moment, and they do build up. We have power to make ourselves into beings of our choosing. If we make wholesome choices in the direction of our aspirations, someday we will wake up and it will be revealed to us that we are even better than we aspired to be. What better reward? I do not promise that building mobiles will make you a better person. Just having desired to build mobiles and having read this far you have done better than most; you are already on the path. Actually constructing something may bring you further along some vision of improvement.

To succeed at any artistic endeavor requires that you enjoy the process. If the feel of the tools and materials is unpleasant, this is not a path to satisfaction. At this point, if the gentle reader has not already done so, I suggest paging through the rest of the book and looking at the pictures. If they look like satisfying tasks to master, then continue.

One last watchword. Making hanging mobiles with delicately balanced horizontal elements is not a path to financial success. I suspect that if a person took the time needed to construct mobiles and used it instead to diligently collect and recycle empty beverage containers, that person would wind up with more money in the bank than the happy soul who was constructing mobiles.

"Jump For Joy" mobile by Bruce Cana Fox

First Mobile, Lightweight Sample

In this section we will construct a simple mobile of one horizontal element and one vertical element, to explore the basic concepts.

Principles first

Let us start with the main balancing method. Take a straight rod and a loop of twine or thread to find the balancing point, *move toward the low side.* That's it. When balancing, move the loop toward the low side. On a horizontal element, move the balance mark toward the low side to find the balance point.

Secondly, *start at the far end and move toward the ultimate support as you assemble the mobile.* There will be many more tips and methods as we proceed, but these two are the guiding principles.

Recipes start with a list of ingredients

This is no different. You will need the following *materials*: **sheet metal,** and **wire or welding rod,** a **block of wood,** and a **wooden pencil with an eraser.**

Next, the *tools* you will need: **sheet metal cutters,** a **drill** and a means of turning the drill, a **punch, round nose pliers, long nose pliers,** a **file.**

Ingredients and Tools

The **sheet metal** and **welding rod** are accompanied by the tools. Almost any way of turning the **drill** is acceptable; one need not have a funky old egg beater style hand cranked drill, but it will work. The **file** should be a medium cut, not too fine, not big and raspy. You need both the **long nose pliers** and the **round nose pliers**; small round nose pliers can be purchased at many of the bead stores that have cropped up. The **punch** does not have to be a fancy automatic style as shown; a sharp nail will work. There are many styles of **sheet metal cutters;** the compound aircraft-style shown are inexpensive and easy to operate, but many other styles of tin snips or heavy scissors can be used.

The **sheet metal** should be relatively thin. Pie tin metal or the aluminum flashing found in home improvement stores will be good for this exercise. Sheet copper, brass, or tin will work too. The rest of the book will concentrate on aluminum, but for this sample mobile, other metals will serve. The sheet metal should not be thicker than .5mm or .020".

The **wire** to use should be moderately stiff: about 1.5 mm or .060". Once again, many different materials will work, but in selecting wire do look for stiffness. I find that aluminum welding rods for heliarc work very nicely.

There are many methods of cutting sheet metal. In this exercise we will use small **tin snips or heavy duty scissors**.

The **drill** chosen should be just a tiny bit larger than the wire. Obtaining the drill may require a trip to the hardware store with a bit of the chosen wire. As a test, drill a hole in the sheet metal and see that the wire can be inserted through the hole with a little clearance.

And so we begin. Cut out the shapes, as shown.

Cutting Sheet Metal: Try to keep the curves smooth. In another step we will file the edges, but try not to make too much work for yourself in either this stage or the filing stage. If you leave too many rough corners in the cutting stage, it makes for much filing. But because you have to file in any case it doesn't do to get too fussy with the snips, either. Here is another case of finding the middle path.

Two Shapes: One is vaguely elliptical and the other a bit teardrop shaped. We will work on design later. For this basic exercise, make them look something like this in roughly this size.

File the shapes smooth as shown. Just for safety's sake, make sure that you aren't creating a knife edge with the file. You have to handle these pieces some more, and finger ends add nothing to mobiles.

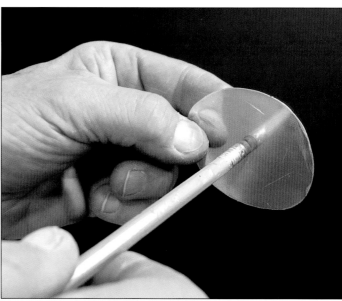

Marking the Center: Once the disk has balanced on the eraser end, do not move the eraser from that position. Backing up the disk with a finger or two, twist the eraser at the center point.

Filing the Shapes: Smooth the contour and then go around with the file nearly parallel to the sheet and remove the burr from the edges. File both shapes.

Find the center of your horizontal element. Balance the horizontal element on the eraser end of the pencil. Mark the center by twisting the eraser into the metal surface.

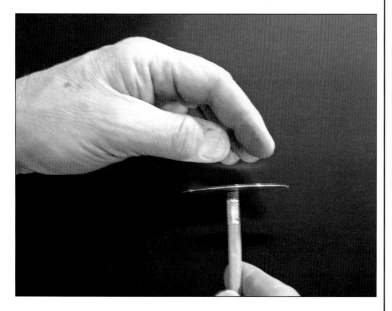

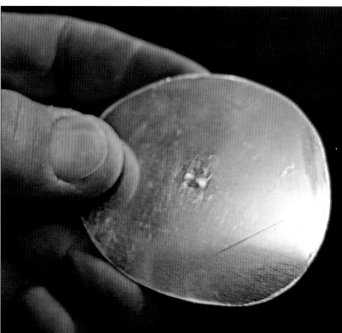

Center Mark: The eraser has made a circle at the balance point of the horizontal element.

Finding the Center: Using the nearly flat eraser end of a standard pencil, move the horizontal element about until it balances on the end of the eraser.

Next construct a wire loop in the middle of a short length of wire. Then bend the ends down as shown.

Starting the Bail: Grasp the middle of a short section of the welding wire with the round nose pliers.

Bend Down: Using the long nose pliers, make relatively sharp bends bringing the legs to parallel.

Wraparound: Take one end at a time and wrap it around the round jaw of the pliers.

Trim Legs: Cut the legs off a bit less than the width of the bail.

The next step is to mark, punch, and drill the holes for the bail. The holes must be placed centered on opposite sides of the eraser mark. The holes will determine the orientation of the element. *It is easiest to put the holes in perpendicular to the desired orientation.* That is, if you want the long axis of the element to be aligned with the direction of the hanger rod, then the holes should be oriented at right angles to the long axis.

Hole Marks: A fine-point marker helps pinpoint the exact spot to punch and drill.

Punch Mark: To keep the drill from skipping about and drilling in a place other than our planned mark, we take the extra step of putting a punch mark or dimple right on the dot. This guides the drill. Pictured is an automatic push down and snap type punch, but a big nail will work. Try to keep the dimple smaller than the hole to be drilled.

Drill: There are many paths up the mountain, there are many ways to turn the drill, from push drills to milling machines. *Using a sharp drill is the key.* If your drill is dull and you haven't learned drill-sharpening magic, buy a new drill and keep it for the mobiles.

Insert the bail into the holes and then bend the legs inward, crimping the legs firmly with the long nose pliers. If your pliers are not long enough to reach the center of the element size you chose, tap them flat resting the bottom on a firm surface and tapping lightly with a small hammer. For these small mobiles, the plier technique is usually adequate.

Insert Bail: If the holes did not exactly match up with the ends of the bail, fear not, there is a bit of play in the bail. Insert one leg and push or pull the other one until it goes in the hole. If this mismatch is too big, you should be able to feel that. If it is close, use the long-nose pliers to press the legs into the holes, stretching or compressing the bail in the process. If you are way off, try making a new bail. At this point you have less invested in the bail than the sheet metal element.

Bend Legs: A little overlap is acceptable in the legs, Align the legs next to each other rather than on top of one another.

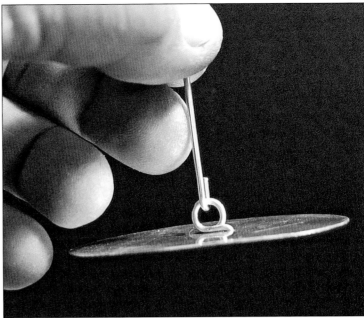

Test the Balance: Using the same wire to test the balance as will be used to connect the elements eliminates surprises later on.

Crimp Legs: This is the long-nose plier technique. Tapping them down is acceptable too.

Now take a length of the welding rod or wire used for the bail and bend a hook in the end of it with pliers. Pick up the completed element and see how it hangs. Every once in a while it will hang level. Most of the time, not. The example shown is not level and will have to be adjusted. Two secrets here. One is that *initial perfection is not required*. The other is that *gentle adjustments are normal* and *creeping up on the level point with more than one adjustment is easier than trying to get it perfect on the first twist*. Move the ring gradually toward the low side until it hangs level.

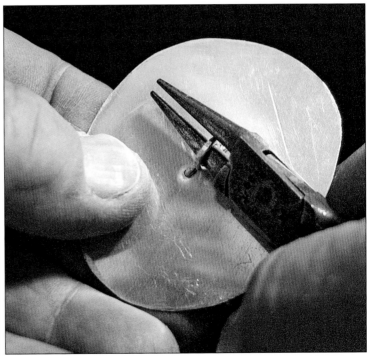

Moving the Ring Along the Leg Axis: Using the same round nose pliers we made the ring with, push a plier jaw into the ring until snug. Then, gripping the element firmly, rotate the ring toward the direction that was hanging low. Then test the balance again.

Having completed and balanced the horizontal element, let us mount the vertical element. Start by cutting a piece of rod or wire a couple of inches (or several centimeters) longer than the desired separation between the elements. Then bend a squarish leg in the end. Mark the end of the vertical element, then punch, drill, poke, and fold to affix the rod to the element.

Estimating and Cutting: Lay the two elements upon the bench the distance apart they should be upon completion. Take some rod and extend it some distance beyond the attachment point of one element, and cut it off some distance beyond the attachment point of the other.

Moving the Ring Across the Leg Axis: Using the long nose pliers grasp the whole of the ring and tilt it toward the side that was hanging low. While grasping the element firmly, you should apply some torque until you just feel the bail barely move. Then test again.

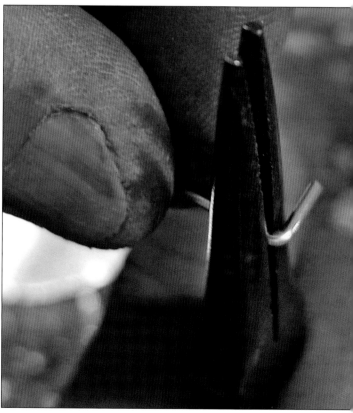

Balanced: After a couple of rounds of slightly rolling and tilting the ring, the element should hang level. Often it is helpful to line it up with some horizontal object in the workshop such as a windowsill.

Bending: Make a squarish little 'J' with moderately sharp corners in the end of the rod.

Marking the Vertical Element: At the pointy end of the vertical element, not far from the end, lay down the 'J' end of the rod and mark where the two holes are to be drilled. As before, punch the marks and drill the holes.

Bend the Short Leg: Push the short leg toward the center of the element. Let the end of it be on one side or the other of the long end, not directly up against it.

Inserting the Rod: Push the long end of the rod through the hole closest to the center, and the short end through the hole nearest the end. The pliers may be needed to help the 'J' part in.

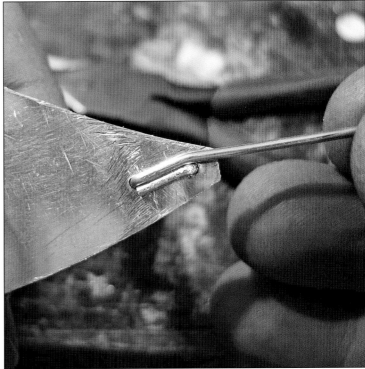

Bend the Long Leg: Now push the long leg over toward the point end and allow the two legs to lay alongside each other. Crimp down with the pliers.

Both elements are now ready to be joined. Make a loop in the end of the rod attached to the vertical element. Don't close the loop yet, it will take a few attachments and detachments before we are done. Attach the newly made loop of the vertical element to the bail of the horizontal element. Find the balance point of the two elements on the vertical element's rod. Then make a loop at that point. This one is a bit counterintuitive, but if you will follow the photos, you see a bit of geometric magic.

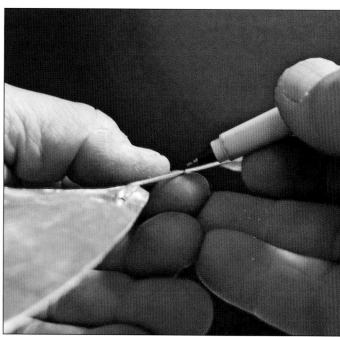

Mark the Balance Point: An ultra-fine marker is good to place a little dot at the balance point. A pencil will work, but the indelible ink will make a mark that is easy to see and hard to rub off with handling.

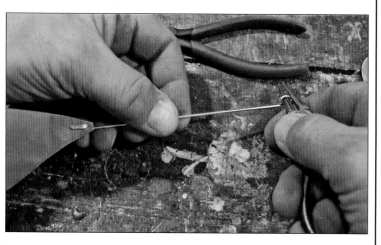

End Ring: With the round nose pliers roll up a ring on the underside of the far end of the vertical element rod. Leave a small gap in the ring for connecting to the horizontal element.

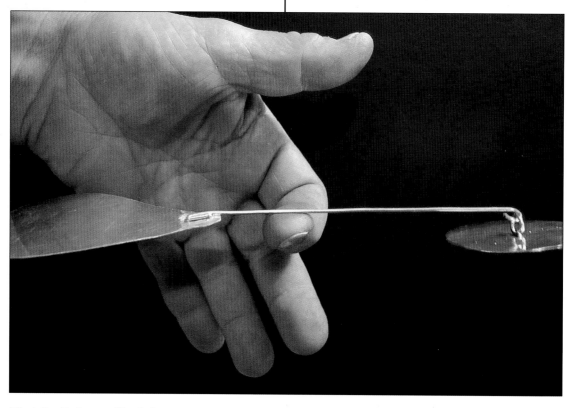

Find the Balance: Hook the two elements together and slide the pair back and forth on a single finger until they look balanced.

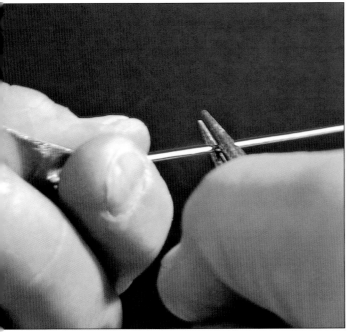

Prepare to Bend: Place the round nose pliers on the balance mark. The bend will be made over the top side.

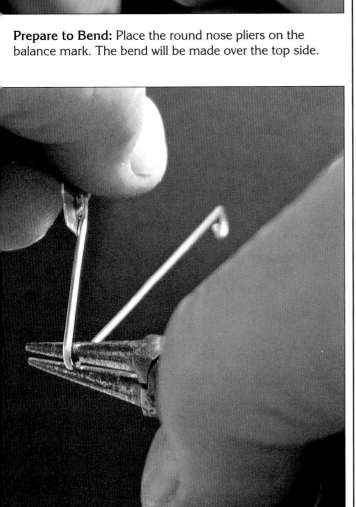

First Bend: Take the vertical element end and bend it all the way over the top of the plier jaw until it is parallel with the loop end.

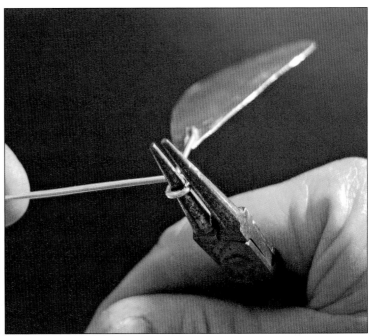

Second Bend: Without releasing the plier grip bend the loop end of the rod back over the top jaw in the same half circle manner as the first bend until the rod is straight.

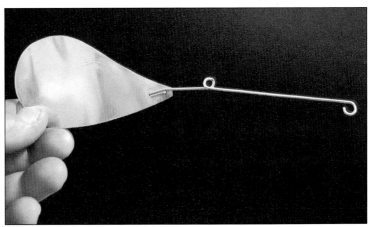

Vertical element: And now you have a loop in the top side of the rod of the vertical element, close to the balance point.

To finish this exercise, all that is left is to balance the mobile. The first placement of the vertical element loop is almost never perfect. Much of this inaccuracy is due to the rod being reduced in length by having the loop made of itself. Experience will allow you to estimate this error and compensate for it by placing the round nose pliers off the mark in one direction or another before wrapping the loop. Even then, adjustments will almost always be needed.

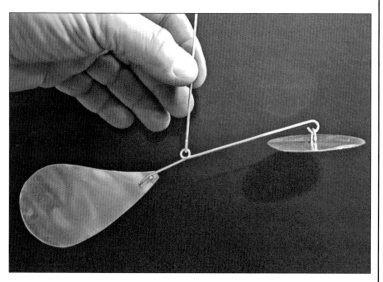

Balance Test: With the hooked wire lift up the two elements by the vertical element rod ring. It appears that the vertical element is hanging low.

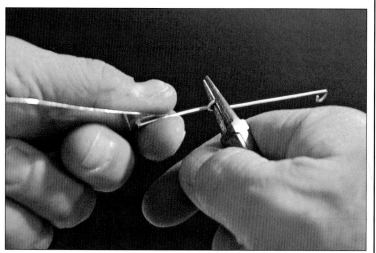

Adjusting the Ring: To raise the vertical element in the balanced pair, roll the ring toward the side that was low. Place the bottom jaw of the round nose pliers firmly in the loop. Holding the rod or element that was on the low side, twist the pliers toward that low end. This has the effect of rolling the loop toward the low side.

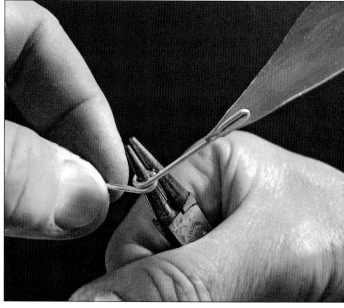

Straightening: Having rolled the ring to the low side, the other end of the wire followed it along. Now bend that wire back until it is straight. Discontinuities in the bent back portion can be corrected with the round nose and long nose pliers.

Now balanced, the two-element mobile exercise is finished.

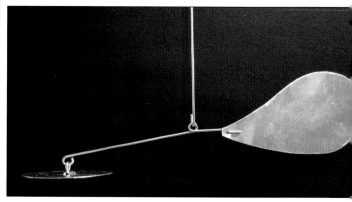

The Finished Two-Element Mobile Exercise

A two-element exercise is perhaps a bit minimalist for most of our tastes, but this technique can be used to build more elaborate designs. Hung from the ceiling with a thread and a push-pin, it will dance in the slightest movement of air. It is, however, a bit delicate and requires special handling and no big winds. Another ongoing use of this technique may be as planning for a larger mobile. As such, this simple attachment technique would allow a scale model of a larger concept to be made in order to work out the relationships of the elements without a large investment. The main value is that in one simple exercise we have learned the basics of balancing the elements and balancing their combination.

Chapter 3

Materials

Mobiles have been constructed of an almost endless list of materials. Junk is popular for some mobiles. Some will go to the lengths to paint the junk hanging from the strings. In this volume we pursue a more deliberate approach. Before cutting metal and balancing the elements realized, one must first obtain relatively fresh materials. Almost all metropolitan areas have metal sales stores that sell everything from tiny pellets of one metal to giant structural shapes of another. Hardware stores deal in sheets and rods of a limited selection of metals. Some large facilities servicing the construction industry will not deal in the quantities an individual sculptor desires. Others deal only in steel.

The first element of obtaining the metal is to find a dealer that has the metals desired, in the quantity you desire and is willing to sell a small amount. Web searches, phone directories, and a few calls later the sculptor will be ready to make a visit. The real high value target at some metals centers is the remainder and cut off racks. A large company may have come in and ordered 43 sheets of aluminum sheet cut to a particular length less than the full sheet size in stock. For that kind of order, the metal service center will chop the sheet to size, package it on a pallet and deliver it to the well heeled customer. They take the ends that were cut off and sell them for less than the going rate for the whole pristine sheet. This is worth looking for for the beginner. An added advantage is that those sheets are in a size that the artist might be able to handle easily and then one does not incur an extra charge for cutting.

Aluminum sheet in the cut-off rack

A service center friendly to the small user will often precut some sheets to easily handled sizes and make those available.

Pre-cut aluminum sheets in various sizes

For the mobiles described here, aluminum sheet, not the softest temper, between 1 mm (.040") and 2 mm (.080") thick, will work best. This size range is not so thin as to look flimsy in a large element, and not so thick as to cause difficulty in cutting. Aluminum comes in various "tempers," refering to how stiff the sheet is. The lowest temper, sometimes referred to "as cast," is pretty pliable stuff on which dings show up immediately. The hardest tempers are extremely stiff and become a chore to cut with anything other than a band saw. When selecting the sheet, feel a variety of different tempers and select one that appears in the middle.

If the sheet being selected is of low price because of a ding or scratch on it, try to visualize how many mobile elements you can get out of the sheet working around the deformity. It might be a good deal.

Also, aluminum comes in a mind-boggling variety of numerically indicated alloys and treatments. For the purposes of this book you can ignore the numbers. Thickness and stiffness are all you need to care about. Bear in mind that many of the people working at the metal service center have gone to great lengths to learn the characteristics of each of the designations. It might improve your relationship with these folks to listen for a while and be appreciative of their expertise so they will help you when you ask, "Do you have something in this thickness but a little stiffer?"

Some sheet aluminum can be obtained at hardware stores. Their selection is usually limited, and the price, when worked out to a per-weight basis, is pretty high. It is worth looking at, but with rare exceptions, a center specializing in metals will be worth the trip.

Another path to sheet metal possession is mail-order. With some combination of catalog or electronic ordering one may obtain smaller sheets of aluminum. The

two disadvantages are expense and touch. This is the one way to pay more for a sheet of aluminum than in a hardware store. Not being able to touch the metal before buying it is an even more serious drawback. Touch is an important part of this art. After you have cut a variety of thicknesses and stiffnesses of sheet aluminum, you are very likely to have developed a preference for a certain feel of the metal. If you live on a remote island or above the arctic circle, mail or computer order might be the best choice. For the rest of us, it is best to pull the sheet off the rack and feel the flex of it.

All of this is three-dimensional. There are flat elements cut from sheet metal that look two-dimensional. The third dimension— the thickness of the metal— is the part that doesn't change much in a mobile. We can pretend to ignore that dimension and call the horizontal and vertical elements two-dimensional. Thinking much the same way about the parts that hold the elements together, think about them as almost one-dimensional. We will take the one-dimensional wire or rod and bend it through another dimension to form rings. The linear wire or rod may even bend under the weight of the mobile parts into an obviously two-dimensional curve.

The one dimension we will worry about when making the connective elements is length. In order to let us do that, we need to put the other dimensions aside by buying wire or rod that can be worked into the shapes we need with the minimum of frustration. Too soft, the wire bends with the weight of the smallest elements. Too hard and the rod is a serious bear to bend. To find the middle path, try and feel many types of wire and rod.

Those who weld aluminum use nice semi-stiff rods of aluminum in a variety of diameters. Establishments that cater to welders and sell them their gasses usually carry a variety of these rods. They are not cheap, but they are very nice to work with, especially in the diameters between 1 and 3 mm (.040" - .125"). Talk nice to the counter person when they are not stressed out with a big order (like a truckload of argon) and they may well let you look at and feel these aluminum welding rods. Beware, some of the rods they sell are not round, and others are embossed with characters that describe the alloy. You want the smooth ones. They are worth seeking out, because these rods are so sweet to work with. The larger diameters (3mm or .125") are nice for making the bails for the horizontal elements. The down side of the welding rods is length. They are only made about a meter long.

For the longer spans in the mobile, it's back to shopping. The metals service center where we found the best sheet often carries aluminum rods 3 or 4 meters (10') long and fairly stiff. A few of these will be just the thing to pick up when buying the sheet stock. You can literally buy rods the diameter of a sewing needle up to bars the size of your thigh. Feel the available rods for diameter, stiffness, and probable difficulty in bending.

Aluminum rod in the rack

A nice mobile can be made using straightened coat hangers. Straightening coat hangers is enough of a drag to make the most skinflint artist part with some money for nicer rod and wire. Sometimes found rod or wire might work for a while, but you may well discover that once you work out a technique with the found stuff, then you can't find any more of it.

Steel welding rod can also be used for mobiles. There is nothing wrong with it except that it can be very hard to bend. Fence wire, available at hardware stores, is another option. Getting it straight can be a chore, but it is less expensive, available in a few sizes, and easier to find. Occasionally one can find aluminum clothesline or grounding wire at hardware stores. This can be a nice alternative too, but be careful, since some of it is plastic coated and others are actually hollow. You really do want a solid wire or rod. Sometimes copper wire can be found, but it is generally more expensive and softer than the aluminum.

Finishing the mobile brings up another material requirement. While some will just sand the aluminum, or others leave it in its natural (as purchased) state, this volume describes painted mobiles. To paint the mobile elements we will have to prepare the surfaces, prime them, and then apply paint.

Once again, there are many ways to get paint on metal elements. After a few mobiles have been completed, the artist may want to experiment with different finishes. One complete method is described here. The materials required are sandpaper, solvent, and spray paint.

Sanding the mobile elements is best done with sandpaper made to be used wet. Both fine and very fine grits should be in your kit for this art. There are many solvents, all of which require care in storage and use. Denatured alcohol is one, acetone another, and there are more. With all of these solvents use them in a well ventilated place with rubber gloves and a respirator designed for solvents, and store them capped in a safe place away from any ignition sources.

The most important consideration in choosing paint is to use paint of one type from a single manufacturer. Pick a brand that can be easily obtained so that when you run out of flat white, it does not mean a major expedition in order to finish a mobile. A couple of spray cans of flat white and a can each of the element colors desired should be enough to finish a couple of medium sized mobiles. Once again, use the respirator when spraying the paint and store the paint properly.

The other connective tissue of these mobiles is rivets. Not used in the sample mobile, they are another separate aluminum material. Like the round nosed pliers, the rivets are not found at the neighborhood hardware store. Pop rivets, with their distinctive little donut head can be found, but it is very difficult to make the bottom of a horizontal element smooth with those pop rivet donuts sticking out. Here we are using a more original style rivet with a flat countersunk head. This style of rivet can be painted over and often made invisible on the flat head side of the element. Rivets can be fashioned out of soft wire, but since very nice ones are actually available, I recommend buying a supply by mail order and spending more time on design of mobiles than perfecting the manufacture of rivets. The supplier is listed in chapter 19.

Other materials can be used for the linear parts of the mobiles. The aluminum is recommended because of the ease of working it.

Chapter 4
Tool Selection

Some woodworkers have been heard to say, "You can never be too thin, too rich, or own too many clamps." Too many tools might come to be a distraction to a mobile artist, but it is hard to imagine how many tools that might take. In this chapter a minimum set of tools is described for going on to a more complex mobile than we constructed in chapter 2.

The first necessary article is a workbench. Shelves worth of books have been written about the bench. All that is required for mobiles is a sturdy bench that won't move about with some hammering, and that can take a few dings and drill holes without causing any trauma. The dining table is usually a bad choice. Even the kitchen table should be off limits for this work.

This art needs time and space, even as the finished product defines space and moves in time. To take the time for mobile construction, the choice and position of the workplace is important. One should obtain or construct a heavy bench, place it out of the traffic pattern of the household, and insure that neither the bench nor the place the bench occupies is held dear by any other member of the household. This allows the articles and detritus of metal work to be laid out and left undisturbed. It is difficult enough to do this work, without having to put everything away until the next session. The space on the bench should be enough to lay out most of the mobile under construction. The ideal height of the bench is just about your belt buckle height.

This **bench** is constructed of 2x12 and 4x4 lumber and is located in the garage. This level of sturdiness might be overkill for constructing mobiles; it does, however, stay put with any amount of hammering.

Next up, a vise. All the way through this mobile construction, work will need to be held in place while the other tools described below are applied to the work. The vise is nearly indispensable. One can use clamps to hold the work to the bench, or even try to hold the work down with one hand while the applying the file or drill with the other. That gets old fast. Balinese mask makers sit on a dirt floor and hold the wooden mask with their bare feet while chiseling or carving with a crooked knife. This is not a path either for either making mobiles or keeping toes attached. Get a vise. It doesn't have to be an expensive one. Actually, a old one picked up at a garage sale will do just as well or better than the shiny store bought model. Pick a large vise. There must be a vise that is too big for mobile making. Surely they make one, but it will be hard to find.

Swivel or not? Many vises are made to turn on their base. As long as the turning mechanism can be locked firmly, there is no reason to deny this small luxury. If one mounts the vise on the corner of the bench so that the artist can step around and approach the work from many angles, the swivel is not needed.

The vise should be bolted firmly to the workbench. What we are looking for here is for there to be no movement at all between the vise jaws and the floor below the workbench. And mount the vise so that the level of the work will be about elbow height.

The mobile maker also needs a way to pad the jaws of the vise to avoid marking the sheet metal. Plywood cutouts are good enough to begin with. Leather, soft metal, or wood can work just as well. The principle here is to keep the rough inner surface of the vise jaws away from the sheet metal.

A large **vise** is firmly connected to the workbench, in this case by its own base clamped to a leg of the bench.

Wooden jaws grip the aluminum without marring. These jaws also raise the work up to a convenient working height. A spacer is seen at the base of the extended jaws to allow gripping work of different thicknesses.

Mobiles of this sort require the cutting of sheet metal. Aluminum sheet can be cut in many ways. The simplest way is with tinsnips.

Aircraft-type, compound-action tin snips can be obtained for cutting straight, curved right, or curved left paths.

Heavier sheets of aluminum can be cut by large tinsnips mounted in the vise for extra leverage.

Large tinsnips. A long pair clamped in the vise for extra leverage. This is sometimes called the "poor man's Beverly."

The maximum convenience for shearing is the Beverly shear. Expensive to purchase new, not easily found used, the Beverly has geared jaws for maximum force on thick sheets.

A used **Beverly shear** clamped to the bench. A fine tool that will give decades of service to a mobile artist.

Another way of cutting sheet metal is with an electric nibbler. Manual ones are available, but the work is so time consuming with the manual nibbler that it will discourage the mobile artist who has much cutting to do. The main disadvantage with the power nibbler is the little curved chunks that spill from the cutting head. Some of them are pointy little arcs that stick to shoe soles and are can be tracked into places where bare feet can be injured. Still, for dividing a large sheet of metal, the power nibbler is hard to beat. There are power shears available also. They might well prove effective for large work. In general the nibblers and power shears are not suitable for closely following marked contours or making careful curves.

Electric nibbler at work.

The bandsaw is a good tool for aluminum cutting. Big, noisy, and expensive, but when fitted with a fine toothed narrow blade, one can cut close to a marked contour. The principle reason for including the bandsaw is that many craftspersons already have a bandsaw. A fine blade in a bandsaw originally used for woodworking will do nice work cutting sheet aluminum.

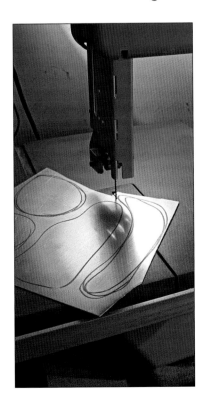

A **bandsaw** at work cutting aluminum sheet with a fine blade.

Metal cutting bandsaws are manufactured to cut a variety of metals. The metal cutting bandsaw runs at a variety of low speeds. They are normally much more expensive than the popular woodcutting variety. As long as the mobile artist sticks to aluminum, they are not needed. If one gets exotic and wants to do stainless steel, or is seduced by the lower price of sheet steel, a different bandsaw, with those much slower speeds will be required.

Cutting sheet metal on a bandsaw is a noisy, messy business. Wear ear and eye protection, every time. Also, be mindful of others and restrict your very loud cutting to the hours when neighbors and family members are not trying to sleep and be mindful of nearby folk trying to hold meaningful conversations.

The artist needs to make holes in the metal; many holes, precisely placed. Drills of the correct size are needed and a way of holding and turning them.

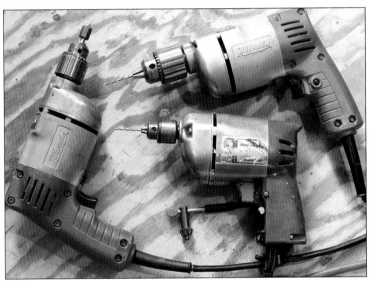

A **brace of drills** is shown, one each for different sizes of holes and one for the countersink. Having a drill motor for each different drill bit used in a given piece of work is extremely handy. It is worth haunting pawn shops for nice used drill motors to gain this extra efficiency.

Another generator of big tool lust is the drill press. For drilling many holes of the same size it cannot be beat for convenience and precision. It might well be overkill for the beginning mobile artist, but if one already owns one from some other craft practice, it can be very handy.

The ordinary drill has been shown and discussed in chapter 2. Now we need to consider the countersink in addition to the twist drill. After a hole the proper size for the shank of the rivet has been drilled, we need to make the outer portion of the hole cone shaped in order to accept the cone shaped head of the flat head rivet. One of the best countersinks for this purpose is the single flute countersink. Multiflute countersinks work well enough but the operation of the single flute model is smoother. If the artist already has a countersink, use that one, if one has to be purchased, make it a single flute. If you are using a multiple fluted model and experience chattering or rough finished holes, try a single flute.

A flat piece of **mild steel**, sanded smooth, used for flattening and setting rivets in aluminum.

Single and multiple flute countersinks with a twist drill index.

own hand for heft and feel the swing of them. Be comfortable with your hammer. You may well purchase and set aside quite a few hammers before finding ones that feel right for the work. Second hand stores and swap meets are great places to explore the fit and swing of various hammers.

Tinner's hammers and a short handled sledge-type hammer. Thor would be right at home with the large one!

There is much bashing of rivets and flattening of aluminum sheets to be done. One needs a surface to work against. The blacksmith uses an anvil. And a large blacksmithing anvil is a wonder to behold and use. Fortunately, since the mobile artist is setting aluminum rivets and flattening aluminum sheet, he or she need not go to the expense of the heavy forged, hardened, and polished steel anvil. A piece of mild steel, flattened and sanded will do nicely. A metal sales center will usually have cut off sections of mild steel. Sanding the surface of such a flat chunk will provide all the surface needed for aluminum work.

To match with the anvil, there are hammers. They come in a profusion of shapes and sizes. Only two are needed to start. A smallish hammer for setting rivets and adjusting bails complements the more substantial short sledge used to flatten elements that have been bent in cutting or trimming. The exact shape of the hammers are not terribly important. The large one needs a wide flat head for flattening. Try various hammers in your

Another oft repeated process of mobile construction is cutting rods and wire. The diagonal cutters are the standard tool, but there are cutters on a variety of other plier shaped tools. Vise grips, fence pliers, parallel jaw pliers, and others can cut wire as well. Likely as not the reader already owns something to cut wires and rods to length. This is another one of those tools that the mobile maker may not have to rush out and buy right away.

Making a nice square end of the rods or wires that show will come to mind sooner or later after starting this business. Often, to avoid filing, one can saw the larger rods to get a nice end with one tool rather than two.

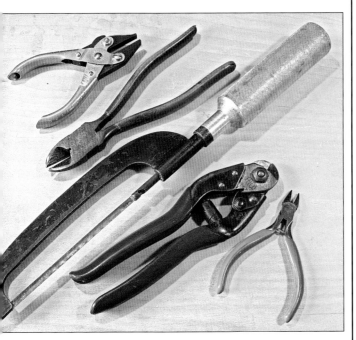

Various **wire cutters**, including a saw for cutting ends off square.

Since the reader has saved so much money by not having to buy hammers or wire cutters, it is in the plier department that we need to purchase something very specific, just for mobiles. One essential tool is the round nose pliers. I have located the pliers shown at MSC. These are not usually to be found at the big home store or the corner hardware. Now it is special order time. The hugest industrial supply house does actually have these, although it might take some poking around in the catalog to find them. Round nose pliers are essential for the loops and bends in mobile connections. Get a good pair. It is worth the wait for delivery. Larger round nose pliers are made for the blacksmith trade. Once you imagine larger mobiles, make the special order for these gems.

Files are going to be important tools. You might as well obtain new files for this endeavor. Why is that you ask, what is wrong with the files in the bottom of this old toolbox I found out in the garage? Files have very hard teeth, so that about the only thing that can really trash the files are other files. It is very rare that one finds a sharp file laying about. Almost all of them have been stored alongside other files and consequently they have been seriously dulled. Treat yourself. Buy a new half round bastard cut file 20 cm (8 in) long that came right out of the box or blister pack. Then keep it wrapped in cloth or hanging to keep it sharp. Using a sharp file is such a treat, that one might well acquire good storage habits just to keep that treat happening.

Files hanging at the ready. The long one on the right is very nice to have, so if you ever see one, buy it, especially if you find it in its paper wrap in the factory box.

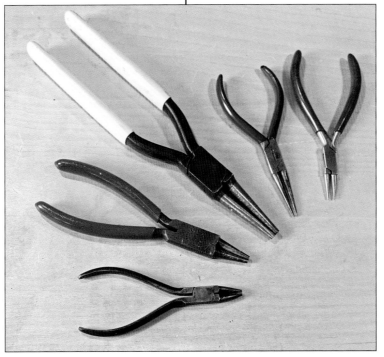

Round-nose pliers. Tiny ones from the sample made in Chapter 2, medium sized general purpose ones that will serve for this book's mobiles, and the large ones from the blacksmith trade.

Then get a similar length half round file in fine cut. Keep these two away from each other and they will stay sharp for a long time. Put handles on them. They're cheap and save your palm and occasionally your toe. The old files from that rusty toolbox? Clean them up a bit and use those to loan out when some else needs a file. Keep the nice ones close.

Also get a file card. It looks like a stiff wire brush on piece of wood. You will be cleaning the file often. Also keep a sharp awl to clean the reluctant stuck bits from the teeth of the file.

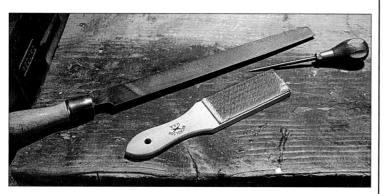

File card and awl. The file can be seen half cleaned. Aluminum will quickly clog the file teeth. After several strokes taking metal off the edge of an element, the mobile maker will need to step back and clean off the file. Brush the chips out of the teeth with the file card, and if there are any really stuck, pick them out with the awl and brush again. This actually speeds the work, as the file makes smoother cuts when the teeth are not filled with aluminum.

Balancing mobile elements requires the artist to put holes directly where the balance mark was laid down. Even as accurate as we can get there will have to be adjustments, so don't try to short cut this part of the process and directly drill the pencil mark. To accurately drill holes, one needs to center punch the hole before applying the drill. There are the very nice automatic center punches and the sort that you strike with the hammer. You can get started with a large nail if need be, but soon the advantage of the automatic punch will become obvious.

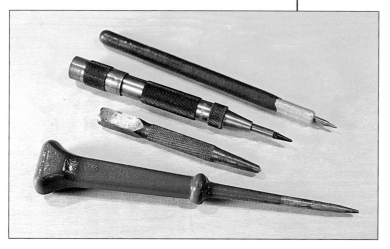

Another process that seems to take too much time, and provide way too little fun is preparing the surfaces to be painted. We really do need to sand everything that has to be painted. This removes blemishes that will show through the paint, removes old paint or factory marks, that can react with the paint we wanted to use, and provides a tooth for the paint to adhere to mechanically.

For sanding, the best is wet-or-dry sand paper, used wet. This can be done by hand, wrapping the sand paper on a block, or using a power sander. Clear the sandpaper often with water spray to keep it cutting. This might remind the reader of the file discussion, and rightly so.

Wet or dry **sandpaper** mounted on an **orbital sander**.

A faster method is with some newer wheel mounted products that look like really stiff scotch-brite. Mounted on a small angle grinder and used with care, these make fast work of preparing flat elements. With the angle grinder use earplugs and eye protection. Also be mindful that the angle grinder with the scotch-brite disk will heat sheet aluminum up to a finger searing heat rapidly. Watch those fingers.

Automatic and manual **center punches**.

For sanding the rods and wires, the wet-or-dry paper is still the best.

When riveting the bails and rods onto the element, it is possible to do the work with just a hammer. A rivet set is a nice to have tool that on one side allows the work to be closed together with the rivet installed, and on the other side, forms a shaped head.

The **rivet set** show was shop-built for 1.5mm (.060") rivets. The hole was drilled slightly larger than the rivet size and the base countersunk. The head forming side was drilled shallow, countersunk and then ground to a round contour. Commercial ones are available, but it is satisfying to make stuff with tools you made yourself.

Angle grinder with scotch-brite disks. The goggles and earmuffs are not just for show. Use them, hear and see into a delightful old age as a sage and respected artist.

And so ends the summary of tools needed to make mobiles. Hopefully the reader has many of these already. Each one of them comes with its own set of mistakes and learning challenges. Making those mistakes and learning from them is a large measure of the work of becoming a mobile artist. As those mistakes occur the first thing to insure is safety. If we ruin a section of sheet metal, we can take that in stride and make a replacement piece. If we ruin a hand, eye, or so much as a finger, it is going to really slow down the appreciation of the artistic process. So be safe, make those mistakes always erring on the side of safety.

Chapter 5
Mobile Design

Having built the two element exercise piece, the gentle reader is ready to embark on a larger piece. This requires a design. Purposely, I did not include plans for your mobiles. Creating the shape in your mind and then on paper is an integral part of the process. I suggest that it is much easier for you to finish your own design than mine.

This is not paint by numbers. I have more confidence in you than that. You can design one on your own, and make it your own statement. Okay, for many of us the first design task might be a bit daunting. Here is a suggestion that will help get the feet wet gently. Look at one of the many books of Calder's works. Find one that has horizontal and vertical elements. Find one that makes you think, "I want one like that!" Make a sketch of it. If the one you are looking at has thirty elements and you find that a stretch, derive one from the picture in its general plan with only eleven or even seven elements. Make a few sketches until you feel good about the potential look of your mobile to be.

Often times a mobile will not look exactly like the sketch when finished. At this point the sketch was just a guide. If the mobile looks good on its own you have not failed. The sketch was just another tool to get you there. After a few mobiles, and experience with the tools and materials, the sketches will converge on the mobiles and your plans will begin to look very like the final product.

A mobile sketch includes the shapes of the horizontal elements, the vertical elements, and the rods between them. Don't plan for where the connecting loops are at this point, just which elements are connected to which

and which rods connect rods and elements together. Draw the horizontal elements flat and the vertical elements flat too. This is a planning document. For the first mobile, or the first few, it might be well to roll out some butcher paper and do a final sketch full size, just to get your arms around the scale that you are considering.

This sketch is your roadmap, reminding you of all the parts to make and the order in which they are to be assembled. When you go to paint the mobile, the sketch will indicate how to reassemble the parts.

After a few mobiles, with confidence building in our technique, it is time to expand our design sense, taking into mind the type of motion we want the mobile to achieve, and the strength and frequency of the breezes in the location for which the mobile is intended.

Another design technique I have used in the past is to cut out many pleasing shapes from the aluminum, and then lay them out on the workbench and shuffle them around until a pleasing arrangement emerges. I usually have to cut another piece or two in order to finish out the emergent design. I don't recommend this for the first few mobiles, but it can be a fun exploration of the form if you don't mind having a few elements that never seem to make it into a mobile. After having done some planned mobiles and gotten some control of the medium, the element shuffle technique can be fun. Having designed a mobile this way, you will still need to make a sketch of it, just in order to be able to reassemble it after painting.

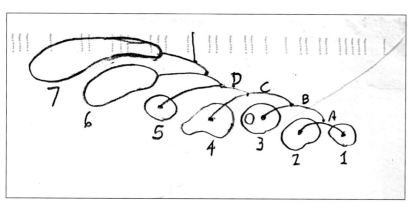

Sample Sketch. Here is a simple, seven-element mobile sketched with no more than you need to proceed to making it. The elements with wires coming from the centers are horizontal elements. The elements with wires coming from the edges are vertical elements. The way I have been working for some time, elements are numbered as shown, and the wires have letters. And, yes, the sketch was done on the back of an envelope. You may already have observed that I was unsure of the shape of the vertical element number 7. If I were to construct this one, I would put off to the metal cutting stage the exact shape for element 7. Shapes are often changed in the cutting or filing stages.

Cutting Elements

Finally the patient reader has made it to the start of the fun: cutting out metal shapes. Tools, trials, materials, design all come together. On a piece of your sheet aluminum lay out the shapes with a magic marker. Don't worry about the color or type of marker, we will remove all of that by sanding or buffing and later on, solvent. Leave a little wiggle room between the laid out elements.

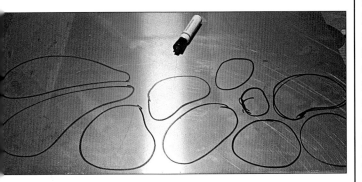

Element shapes laid out on sheet aluminum. The contours may be a bit vague and that is on purpose as the final contour is determined as much by feel as by copying the design.

It is best to make the cuts in two stages. A rough cut just to bust the element out of the sheet and then a cut close to the contour. Most of the snip type tools behave better when trimming a narrow waste piece rather than a wide section.

When you laid out the element with the magic marker on the sheet, you spent a bit of time interpreting the design. As you are cutting out the element, you have it in your hands and are now re-interpreting the design. This cutting time is also design time. Now is the time to get closer and closer to the contour and the shape of each element. Now is the time to make the elements relate to one another in shape. Rather than slavishly copying a traced out shape, this cutting is establishing the shape. The forces of pushing the shape and operating the tool are making the contour. Ideas about the feeling of curves come at this very time, and should be listened to, and expanded upon. If that means that you mess up an element, worry not. Cut down the ugly element to be a smaller element for this or another mobile. You can cut again. The sheet metal didn't cost *that* much. The learning of the shapes and the dance of the tool carving into the aluminum are more important.

Elements laid out on the bench to assess the design.

Cutting out shapes on the Beverly shear. Observe the waste snippets under the cutting edge and note that they are from the second cutting, the shape having been roughed out first.

Once you have a pile of cut out elements, take a look. Lay them out on the bench in the order of the design. Move the elements around and appreciate how they relate to each other. This is a time of reevaluation of the original design. Do you need another element? Does that big one in the middle unbalance your original vision? Does it cry for another vertical element? Do the curves on those end elements complement each other now? Would they continue to when in motion? There is nothing sacred about your original design at this point. It can be treated as a jumping off point. Need more elements? Cut more metal. Once it looks really fine, stop and make an updated sketch. If you feel particularly good about the arrangement, now might be a time to mark the parts, numbering each element. This might be doubly important if some of them are similar.

A central point of the process of cutting out the elements is that at cutting time, you are spending more time with each element than you likely did in the original design. This is no time to make a distinction between the designer and the craftsperson. In this process, the art effort continues far into the work that others might interpret as drudgery.

Another modern tool, useful at this time in the process, is a digital camera. Make a photo of the arrangement. Just a review on the back of the camera can be enough to remind you of your most pleasing arrangement. This will help later.

In the process of cutting out the elements, many of the tools we use will bend the element slightly. Now it is time to take each element and flatten it. This is when we use that anvil plate. A large hammer can gently move the bent edges back to flat. If the hammer you have is leaving unpleasant marks in the aluminum as you flatten the element, tape a piece of leather to the face of the hammer. If unpleasant marks are coming from the anvil side, is it time to file and sand the anvil to flat.

Flattening the edges of an element with a large plastic faced mallet.

Next it is time to smooth and trim each element. Here we may loose sight a bit of the whole mobile as we refine the curves of each separate element. We can, however replace the element in the arrangement laid out on the bench from time to time to ensure we retain the harmony achieved in the previous rough cutting.

Clamp the element in the protected jaws of the vise. Using the large coarse file, file up and over the curve.

Filing the edges of an element with a large half-round file. Keep the angle of the file to the element edge moving. Sweep the angle of the file around the curve, using your whole body in the movement.

Second in a sequence of just one file stroke.

In this motion we are not just "following the form", but creating the form. Through the face of the file, feel the edge of the element. Feel the discontinuities in the curve, where there is a flat spot or little high spot or corner happening. This motion of raising up one arm

and lowering the other as the file moves across the work, and even twisting the center of the body at the same time, gets the whole body involved in the shape. The more pathways to the brain that you can involve in defining the shape, the better the shape will become for you. While you may have had an initial vision of an element shape in mind, as the mind and body refine that shape, that shape becomes more what you want it to be.

Loosen the vise and turn the piece. Continue with the shaping. Go around twice. Then take the fine file and remove the burr that you created on each side of the element's edge with the large file. This involves holding the file nearly parallel to the face of the element.

The file stroke ends, having smoothed and defined the curve of the element.

Using the fine half-round file to **trim the burr** off the edges of the element. Note the angle of the file.

Take the element out of the vise and feel it. Run your fingers around the edge and feel for any discontinuities that you could not feel through the file. If there are any, clamp the element back in the vise with the discontinuity up and work it over gently with the fine file. Then remove the edge burrs.

Up until now, the description has been for creating convex shapes. Many designs have concave shapes in their elements. Since it is difficult to run the file down into the concave portion, the technique needs to be modified a bit. Flip the file over to the rounded side. Do not use the file exactly perpendicular to the element, but at a more acute angle. The shallower the concave portion, the more the angle can approach parallel to the element edge. In really deep concave portions, the curve of the file may be exactly the curve desired. If the concave portion of the reader's design is even deeper than that, one may have to invest in a round file.

Cleaning the file. The rightmost section of the file is still clogged with aluminum.

The round side of the half-round file cuts and smoothes a concave curve in an element.

Getting good results from a file requires keeping it clean. Use the file card (a kind of very stiff brush) to remove the particles of aluminum that clog the file's teeth. This should be done every eight or ten strokes of the file. This might seem like a waste of time at first, but it is with the clean, working file that we can feel the cutting action forming the shape. The feel is an important part of our design refinement so we need to do the extra little work to keep that feeling. If the file is clogged with filings, it feels as if we are using some sort of bludgeon to beat the work into submission rather than the fine cutting tool that a sharp file really is. Don't waste the

time spent cleaning the file. Look over at the work in the vise, noting where you are into the process for that element and making a little plan for the next move.

[serious digression time] A minister friend of mine gave a sermon on finding time in your life for spiritual work, describing ways to make time in between the mundane tasks of life to do spiritual development. I disagree. I believe that it is all spiritual work. In the same way, when constructing a mobile, which may be spiritual work in its own way, there is almost no time in the process in which you are not doing the artistic work. And so it goes for cleaning the file. [digression mode off]

Once we have our pile of elements shaped to satisfaction, and have laid them out following the design, we need to prepare them for finishing. The aluminum as cut from the sheet is never quite what we want to hang, even if we are looking for that bare aluminum look. While many finishes are possible, this volume instructs for a painted mobile. To prepare the surface for painting we need to clean, flatten, and give it some "tooth". Either wet sanding or buffing with the scotch-brite wheel will do. In cleaning at this stage, we are just getting manufacturing marks and old paint off. We will take care of fingerprints later. The piece gets flattened at this time too. Little humps and nubbins are sanded to flat. The fine sanding or buffing creates tiny groves that the paint can mechanically grip, improving adhesion with what some call tooth.

Preparing for wet sanding.

Spraying off the aluminum bits into a bucket. A time to examine the element for both flatness and a buff look devoid of shiny spots.

Wet sanding an element using 100-240 Wet-or-Dry type sandpaper. Keep the work wet. The danger of electric shock is reduced by using only double insulated power tools with a grounded plug. For absolute electrical safety use a pneumatic sander powered by compressed air.

Buffing an element with the scotch-brite wheel. It is held with one had while the other operates the buffer. This technique requires fairly strong hands and arms. Others may choose to clamp the work down. Another difficulty with the buffing approach is that the motorized wheel tends to heat the element. It just makes the element hard to hold. When that occurs set the element down to cool and work on another.

And that's it. The diligent reader should now have a set of buffed elements laid out on the bench in roughly the order of the design. Now is the time to check the sketch of the mobile and mark the elements according to their position in the mobile. A wipe-off magic marker is handy, but a regular marker or even a grease pencil will do for this purpose. Number the elements as the sketch. If you number all of the horizontal elements on the top side, it will be easier to keep straight which side of the element gets the bail and on which side the holes are countersunk.

Chapter 7

Forming The Bail

The little part that attaches the horizontal element to the rods and wires is called a bail. That is also the name of the wire part of a bucket across the top by which it is carried. The bail is the interface between the horizontal element and the wire element. The relative size of the bail wire and the bail loop helps to determine how much the element can turn in the finished mobile. A tight bail will restrict movement, while a large bail will allow the horizontal element to turn a bit.

The bail in a finished mobile.

This little bit of construction is not difficult but it does involve a number of steps. The reader and beginning mobile artist is encouraged to follow the instructions a few times before attempting to improve on the technique. There must be a better way, but many ways other than this have been tried and this is one way that has worked for some years.

Start with a length of fairly soft 3mm (1/8") diameter aluminum wire about 7cm (2 1/2') long. For really tiny elements, a smaller wire or welding rod can be used. Sand the wire. Bend it into a sombrero shape and flatten the ends. Pound the ends flat, trim and file the ends, then drill holes in the ends to accommodate your chosen size of rivet. What? That's it? That's all there is to it after all that build up about number of steps and technique? Simple enough to state, but there are some complexities. Follow the pictures and build a few.

Start by sanding the wire. The whole adhesion of paint business has us doing all of this sanding. But if we don't want paint flaking off the mobile parts later on, it pays to prepare the metal.

Sanding the wire before bending. Shown is a bitsy scrap of 400 Wet-or-Dry paper. Just pull the wire back and forth, turning until the whole length has a matte finish.

Here is where those round nose pliers we worked so hard to get come in handy. The are about the only way to get these bends done nicely.

The first bend, in the middle, using the round nosed pliers

Turn pliers so the U-shaped piece is to one side of the bend and then **bend the wire back 90 degrees**.

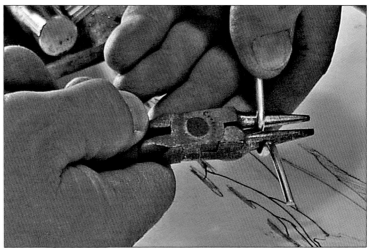

Repeat the bend on the other ear.

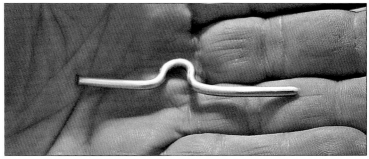

The **sombrero shaped bail wire**, ready for flattening

Flattening one side of the bail on a slightly rounded corner of a vise. The vise corner was just filed to the desired contour to avoid having a sharp corner in the bail profile. The edge of your anvil plate, slightly rounded would do as well. Bang it with the hammer until the flat part is about three times wider than the wire. Come fairly close to the bend with the flat part.

Since the flattened parts are never quite parallel, or even going in the same direction, lightly **clamp the body of the bail** in the vise so the ears are on the top surface of the vise jaws, then **tap with the hammer** until they are parallel with the vise jaw.

The straightened bail, ready to trim

Then use almost any kind of plier to **straighten the now flat bail ears**.

Trim the ends of the bail ears to a bit more than the width of the loop on each side. Then smooth with a file.

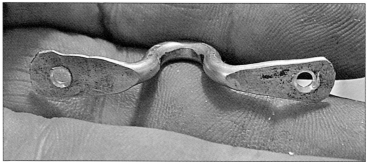

The finished bail. The observant mobile maker may already have noticed that there is some burr and swarf on the edges of the hole shown. Since that side is going up against the top of the flat element, and will be forced flat when riveting the bail to the element, not much time was spent in cleaning. What is important, is for the rivet to fit snugly.

Center punch each ear near the widest part. Then **drill a hole** the size of the rivet you had planned on using.

The bail can be turned into a little jewel of perfectionist craftsmanship, but usually that is not necessary. The bail is on the top on an element that is being looked at from below. It needs to be evenly produced with good craftsmanship, and be satisfying to work with further and look at in the final product, but it is not the main event. The person hanging the mobile is the last to get a good look at the bail. If you have to chose between getting the curve of a horizontal or vertical element perfect and getting the bails perfectly identical and smoothed, err on the side of too much work on shape and edges of the elements.

Chapter 8

Balancing the Horizontal Elements

Now the reader is getting close to the heart of the matter. Balance. It is the center we need to find, mark, and mount the bail above. Each horizontal element has a center of balance and it is possible, necessary, and fantastic to find that balance and make all the elements in our design be level and even. Possible because it is demonstrated below in simple steps. Necessary because it makes the design and allows the shapes to interact without dancing around at odd angles. And fantastic because of the rarity of the practice. Until we have done the balance we can't appreciate why we don't see horizontal elements in the store bought mobiles.

The steps are: find the center, mark the center, mark the bail holes, punch the bail holes, drill the bail holes, countersink the underside of the bail holes, rivet the bail on, check for the center, and finally adjust the bail lengthwise and crosswise to regain the center.

Three-finger balancing technique.

The standard wooden pencil has a nice eraser on the end. On a newer pencil the eraser still has a little flat spot at the top. Push the eraser end of a pencil up between the fingers to the center. With just a bit of rotation and careful adjustment, the element will balance on the pencil eraser. Or you can use the pencil point to make a mark between the three fingers, and then do the balance on (or more likely, very near) the pencil mark.

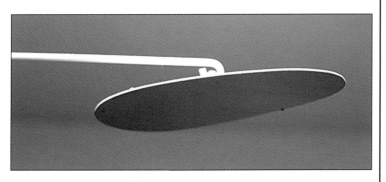

A single balanced element. The ceiling line in the background verifies that the element is on the level.

The first task is to find the center of the element. If you can just balance the element on a finger, you are there. But sometimes, in the shapes we design, it is not immediately obvious where the center is. The three finger technique is used to get close to the center. Balance the element on three fingers. Slowly bring the three fingers together. The element will self adjust during the contraction of its support, and the center will be in the middle of the three fingers. For purposes of marking the center and positioning the bail it is easiest to have the top side of the element facing down while finding the center.

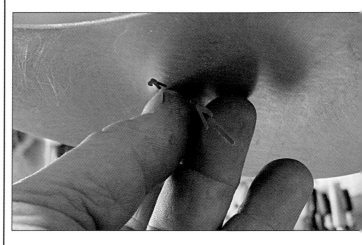

There's the place to **make the mark or place the eraser**.

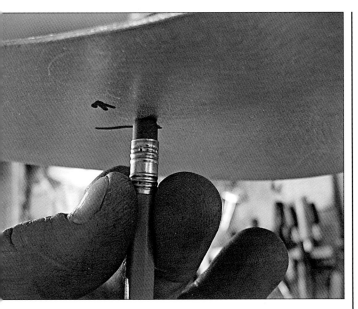

Pencil eraser balance

At this point twist the eraser into the aluminum element without moving it from the center.

Pencil eraser mark in the top of the element. This will not show after painting.

Now position the bail over the eraser mark working to get the highest point of the bail directly over the center of the eraser mark. The bail ears will be perpendicular to the wire or rod that will hold the element. Pay attention to this alignment, as it is a good part of what establishes the relationship between the horizontal elements.

Bail positioned over eraser mark.

Either make a mark with a scribe, pencil, or marker through the bail holes, or center punch through the holes. At this point it is a good idea to make a little mark on the end of one bail ear and the top of the element, in order to line up the same end as you marked or center punched when you rivet the bail to the element. The center punching works very nicely on our steel anvil plate.

Punching the element through the bail holes.

Set the bail aside. If you made marks on the element, center punch those marks. Drill the center punched location with the rivet sized drill.

Drilling the element from the top. In this photo there is a piece of wood backing the drilling operation. The drill is not going into the steel anvil plate.

Then turn the element over and countersink holes at the bottom of the element to the size of the rivet head. Check these holes against the rivet to ensure a good fit. It is a good idea the first few times to drill a scrap piece and check the countersink sizes before boring into our nicely finished mobile element. The fit of the rivet does not have to absolutely perfect. The act of bashing the rivet will take up a tiny bit of mismatch of hole to rivet size, but only a tiny bit. Try this ahead of time too.

Countersinking the rivet hole. In the drilling process, sometimes we find a little bit of metal swarf still stuck to the side of the hole. On the top side of the mobile, it will be covered by the bail. On the bottom side, the countersinking will remove it. When the countersinking is done, though, the edge of the countersunk hole should look nice. If any swarf is left there, scrap it away gently with a knife or other hard tool.

Rivet time. Place a rivet in one of the countersunk holes and place it upright on the steel plate. Place the bail over the rivet and press down. If you have a rivet setting tool, place it over the rivet and tap it to bring the bail and element and rivet together.

Next, cut the rivet off if it extends out as far as the one shown below. The diagonal cutters are adequate to this task. Leave 2 or 3 mm (1/8") showing above the bail. Then pound the rivet flat with the hammer or the hammer and the doming dimple in the rivet setting tool. This is done against the anvil plate. The smoother the anvil plate, the smoother the bottom surface of the rivet will be. If it is being painted, it is more important to have a good fit, than a shiny rivet, so pay more attention to the similarity of the countersunk hole and the rivet's flat head diameter than to the polish. Repeat the process on the other bail ear and element hole. If there is a bit of mismatch on getting the rivet into the bail hole, you can bend the bail in or out a bit to match up with the rivet.

The **bail** riveted to the top of the element. The black marks indicating direction will be removed before painting.

Not so fast. We're not done yet. Fashion a hook from the rod or wire that is going to be used to hang the element. Raise the element from the bench with the hook through the bail and examine how level it hangs. The chances are very, very good that it will not perfectly level. Turns out, no matter how hard we try, the element just won't hang flat the first time. So we adjust. This method of making horizontal elements has some room for adjustments.

Element **top, bail and rivet**. The shop-made setting tool has been used to seat the bail and rivet firmly on the element.

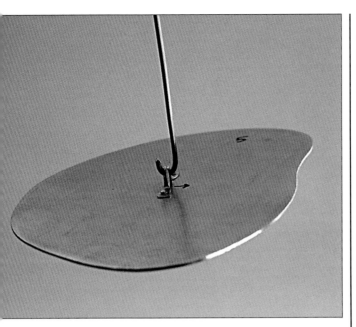

First test of the bail centering. We didn't quite get the bail in the exact center this time.

Let's get the basic principle down again. Move toward the low side. As we move along the length of the bail, we use the hammer (gently). As we move from side to side on the bail, we use pliers. In tapping the bail to move it in the long direction, tap just enough that you can feel the bail move a bit. Then get the hook and test for level. Move up on the correction gently.

Tapping the bail to move it toward the direction that the element tilted low.

First adjust along the length of the bail. When the element is hanging straight along the bail axis, then use the pliers and firmly gripping the bail with the pliers and the element by hand, just barely move the bail. Test with the hook and move again. Sneaking up on the level. Be patient. And be patient with yourself trying to be patient.

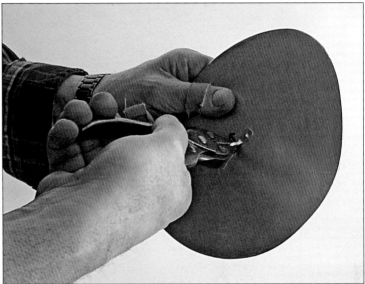

Bending the bail gently but firmly.

You may have to go back to the lengthwise bail movement after adjusting the side to side center. This is normal.

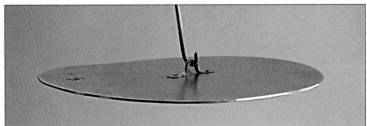

Finished and balanced element.

The main reason for patiently sneaking up on the balance point is the prevention of metal fatigue. If we move the bail back and forth across the center, we can actually work harden the thin parts of the bail and get it to break. Once the bail is hanging level set it down and move to the next one.

Although we done this in a "one at a time" sequence, there is only a little reason not to do elements in batches. That little reason is just that of keeping the bails with the elements they were matched with between process steps. That's why it is shown here going through the process from centering finding to final balance on one element at a time.

Chapter 9

Horizontal Element Connecting Rod

While there is no prescribed order required for elements vertical or horizontal in mobiles, many beginning mobiles have their horizontal elements toward the lower portion and their vertical elements closer to the hanging point. In the balancing and spacing of the mobile we generally work from the bottom to top. So having assembled the horizontal elements and their bails, we will discover the linear elements that connect them.

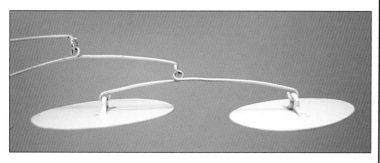

Two **horizontal elements connected** with an aluminum welding rod linear element.

Again, not a hard and fast rule, but a good place to start is with a linear element that has a loop on top for connection to other linear elements, and two loops on the underside connecting either to horizontal elements or to other linear elements.

As our mobile elements are laid out on the bench in the pattern we want to achieve, we can measure the distance between the bails of two successive elements. A harder part is knowing how much wire or rod to cut to achieve that distance. Time to work backwards. Cut a known length of rod or wire, and then bend the three loops in it. Bend these loops with the round nose pliers you will use for that size of rod. Mark it with its starting length. Then you can measure between the centers of the lower loops and subtract (oh, no, you didn't tell me there was going to be MATH in this book!), yes, subtract the distance between the centers from the original length. This figure is what you then add to the distance between the bails to get the length to cut the rod. Get out the calculator if you have to, and write the numbers down. This is much easier than trying to guess the right length.

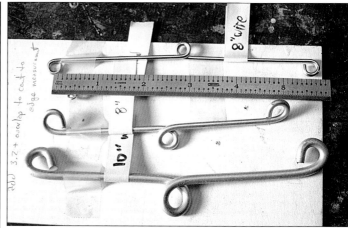

Rods and wires, measured, marked and kept for reference. The linear element sample at the top was bent from an 8" wire. The centers of the lower loops measure 5.6", so the figure to add to the desired distance between two element bails or upper loops is 2.4".

If you have any thoughts of painting the mobile, sand the rod before bending. Paint has a hard time with most rod and wire that doesn't have some tooth to it. Now is the time. It will be way too hard to do once the loops are formed.

The simple job of **sanding the rod before bending**

With the measurement of the desired distance between the bails of the first two elements, add the extra length determined from the sample of rod, and cut the rod to the sum of those two numbers. Bend a loop in each end, in the same direction. Leave a little opening in the loop so a bail can be slipped in.

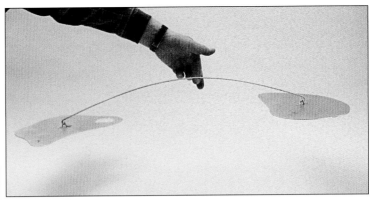

Finding the balance point. Not quite even yet.

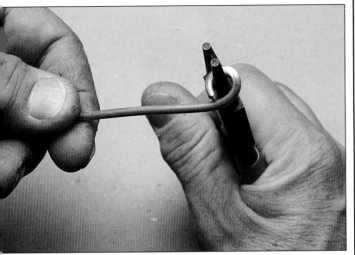

Rolling up an end loop.

Once the balance point is found, mark that point. A small magic marker is nice for this. Then grip the rod at the point of the marked balance point and bend the rod over the plier nose for a half circle.

Bending the second end loop in a linear element.

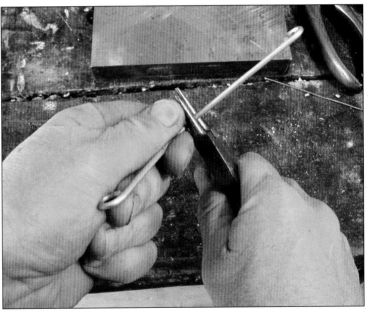

Now take those first two elements and hook one to each end of the linear element. Find the balance point with your finger.

Starting the bend over the marked balance point. This bend is going the opposite direction than the end loops. As the end loops face down, this bend is going up.

The first leg is bent 180 degrees.

Without moving the pliers, grasp the other end and pull it up and over the opposite half circle.

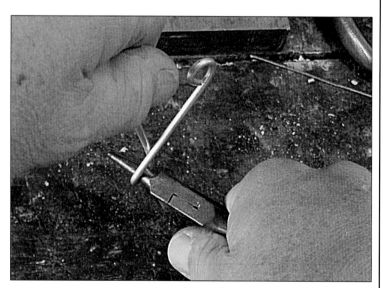

The second end is bent back in the direction the first leg came from, also 180 degrees.

The pliers can then be moved to clamp down on the loop and the legs and the legs can be adjusted to appear even.

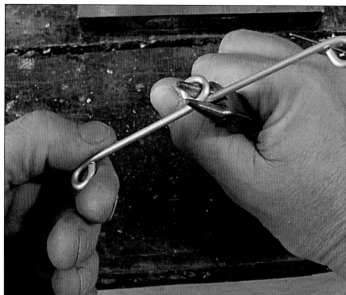

Finishing the top loop bend.

Now take the linear element and hang the two horizontal elements upon it. Use the hook we made for testing the balance of the horizontal elements and pick up the linear element with the two horizontals to test the balance. Don't be disappointed, they are almost never balanced at this point. Note which end is low. Take the horizontal elements off the rod. Hold that low end and place one round nose of the pliers in the loop. Use the pliers to roll the loop toward the low end.

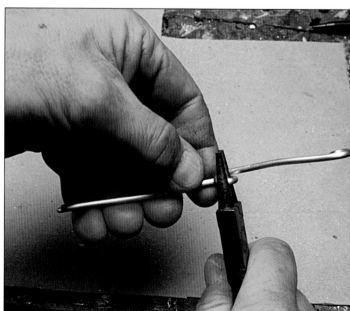

Grasping the loop with round nosed pliers and the low side of the linear element.

 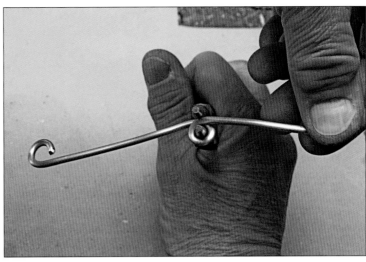

Rolling the loop toward the low side. Hold the low side of the linear element firmly and twist the pliers to move the loop.

With the pliers repositioned, **adjust what had been the high side back down to level**.

Reposition the pliers to grasp between the loop and two legs on the bottom. Pull the other, the end that was the high end, down to straight. Then hook up the horizontal elements and test for level again. Repeat the loop tweaking as needed, slowly sneaking up on the balance rather than over correcting. When satisfied with the first two elements' alignment, place the pair back in the layout of elements.

Assuming that the design calls for more than two horizontal elements in a row, we need to have a different end on the linear element. To make this right angle end loop, start the same way as the straight loop end.

After making an end loop, then center it by bearing the outside plier jaw against the rod and twisting the loop.

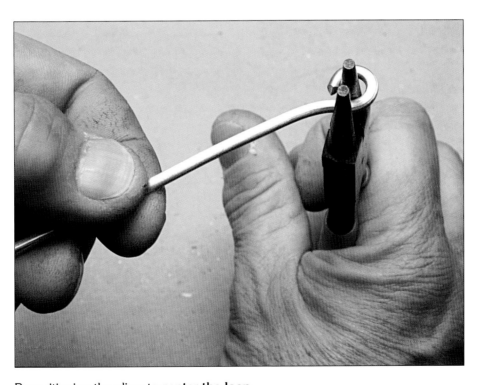

Repositioning the pliers to **center the loop**.

Then bend the loop down, most of the way to perpendicular.

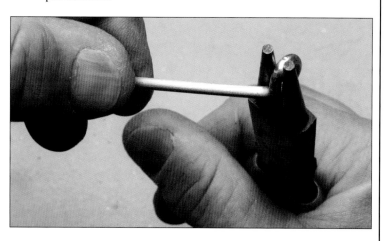

Bending the loop down to make the right angle loop.

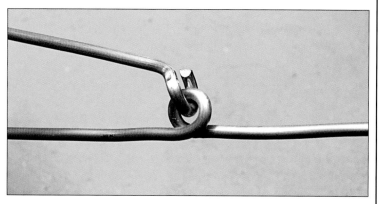

The right angle loop and another linear element running parallel.

As a next step, measure from the open upper loop between the two first horizontal element and the bail of the next element up the chain. Add the extra distance for the bends and cut a rod that length. If the design has elements in a line, put a right angle loop in one end of your linear element and a straight loop in the other end. If you want the linear element connecting the first two horizontal elements at a right angle to the current element, then put a straight loop at each end. Repeat the steps of balancing on the finger and wrapping the upper loop in two steps over the mark. As before, tweak the loop toward the side that hangs lower than you had envisioned.

This is the process for joining and balancing the horizontal elements in your design. Continue in this manner until the planned horizontal elements are all hanging.

As you get to longer spans, a thin rod that you started with may be bending too much for the look you had planned. This is your cue to move to a larger diameter rod.

You may notice as you are balancing more weight on one side of the linear element, and the rod on one side of the upper loop is getting much longer than the other side, that you are having to tweak the loop farther and farther. This is because the loop is taking an equal length of rod from the long side and the short side, and that is proportionately more on the short side than on the long side. In order to maintain the same proportion of lengths that achieved balance before making the loop, you may find it handy to move the pliers a bit toward the long side from the balance mark before bending. It is hard to guess exactly right on this, but it does save some loop tweaking.

Chapter 10

Vertical Element Connecting Rod

The vertical elements do not have to be placed in any set order in a mobile. Some common configurations of mobiles have the horizontal element below and vertical elements above, so they are presented in that order here. Please mix it up and find your own designs.

There are vertical elements that hang down from a rod. There can be vertical elements that hang and swivel. Such designs are relatively simple to implement once the tools and techniques we discuss have be acquired.

A bit more complex are the vertical elements that are fixed to the end of a rod. Designwise, the vertical element can ignore the rod, or can be an extension of

the rod. One can even imagine a vertical element cut to have a long portion that then twists to attach to another element, replacing the linear element.

The first thing to do attaching a vertical element is to measure. As we did with the double ended linear element in the last chapter, we cut a known length, then bend and end loop and a middle loop, leaving one end straight. Then we mark the original length on this test element. The magic number is the difference between the bent length (loop center to straight end) and the original length.

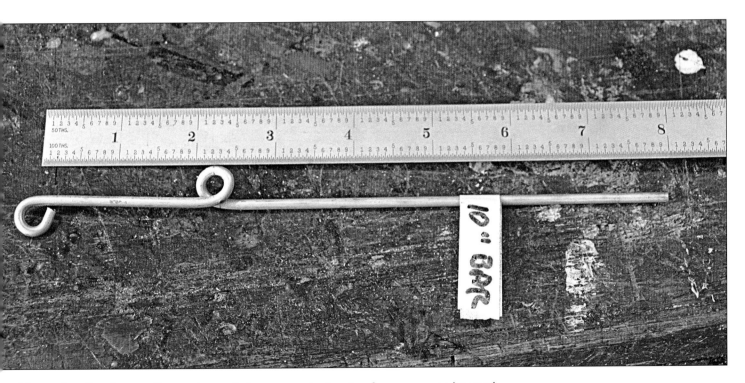

Measuring the dummy linear element. Any convenient units of measure can be used. What is shown is inches and tenths.

Take the lowest vertical element in the design and hold it in the position relative to the rest of the assembled mobile on the workbench. Measure the distance from the center of the top loop to a point 30 - 40 mm (1 1/4" to 1 1/2") into the vertical element. It can be handy to put a pencil mark at that measurement point. To this distance, add the difference between the finished test piece and the test piece's original length. That's how much rod to cut. Don't forget to prepare the rod for painting, assuming that's the plan.

Next make the decision of the type of end ring on the linear element. The straight loop hangs the linear element below at a right angle to the one being constructed while right angle bent loop makes the element below parallel. Construct the loop.

Bend a right angle loop end.

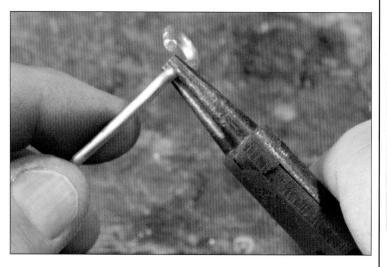

And **bend the loop down** at nearly a right angle.

Next, using the flat anvil plate, pound a section of the straight end flat, to join to the vertical element. It should wind up being about two and a half to three times as wide as the diameter of the rod. Flatten a length about the same distance as that measured inside the edge of the vertical element.

The opposite end of the linear element pounded flat.

Next trim and file the flattened end. There will be a top side with some hammer marks and a bottom side that is smooth from the surface of the anvil plate. On the top side center punch for two holes on the flattened end.

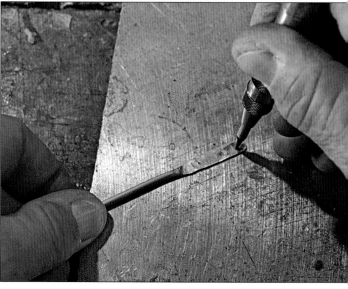

Center punching for the rivet holes. The spacing shown uses most of the flattened area.

Drill for the rivet size and trim the swarf from the hole rim.

Drilling the rivet holes leaves a bit of aluminum on the bottom side of the hole. It can be cleaned up with a relatively coarse file.

Set the flattened and drilled end on the vertical element and mark the hole closest to the edge of the vertical element.

Thin lead mechanical pencils are very nice for marking through holes.

Center punch and drill that hole. "Why not do both holes at once?", the gentle reader is heard to wonder. Doing both holes at once is certainly possible, but it re-

quires that everything be marked very carefully. If we do them one at a time, it avoids many opportunities for errors and redrillings and oblong holes. So drill the one hole and countersink the backside.

Center punch here, too. It is just way too hard to keep a drill centered on a pencil mark. Even a tiny center punch mark will keep the drill from wandering and putting the hole in the wrong place.

This is a countersink job that also has to match up with the size of the rivet head. If you need to, sneak up on the right size by countersinking a bit and then comparing the size of the hole with the rivet head a couple of times.

Then set the rivet in holes on the anvil plate.

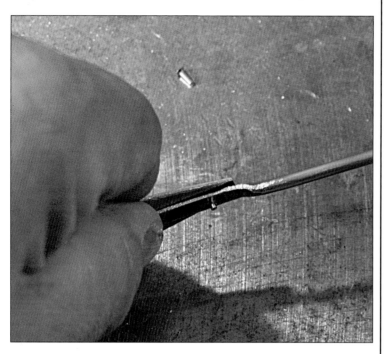

Assemble the holes and the rivet. This view shows a bit of gap between the flattened rod and the vertical element.

Once you place these parts on the anvil plate, **tap them together** or use a rivet set.

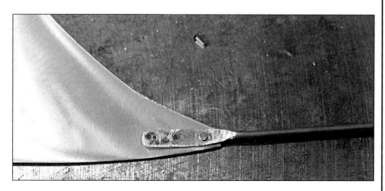

Assembled and riveted, the angle of the linear element can still be adjusted.

The assembly with one rivet holding the vertical and linear elements together can be taken back to the rest of the mobile. We can adjust the angle of the linear element to the vertical element. Then, using the second hole in the flat end, drill the rivet hole in the vertical element. Countersink the back side and then set the second rivet.

Drilling the second hole through the vertical element is easier, because the hole in the flattened rod acts as a guide. It will be in exactly the right place.

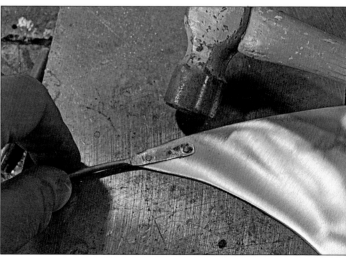

The vertical element is firmly fixed to the linear element.

Now the balancing act. Hook the vertical element and its linear extension to the top of the rest of the mobile and lift it all up. Use the finger to find the balance just as with the horizontal elements.

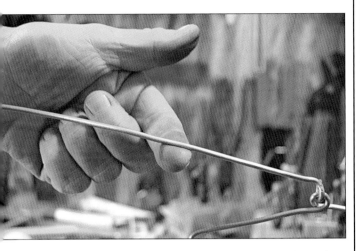

Balanced on a finger. Mark the point just above where the weight rests on the finger.

Mark this point, squeeze the point or an adjusted point with the round nose pliers and bend each end 180 degrees over the plier jaw.

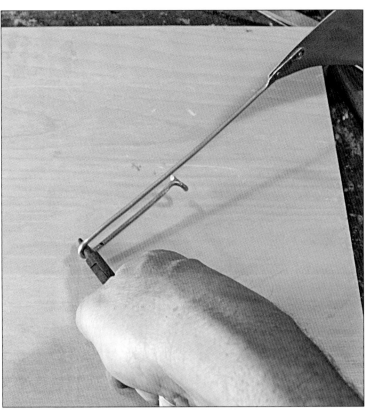

The first bend. Here the long side with the vertical element has been lifted up and over the pliers' round nose.

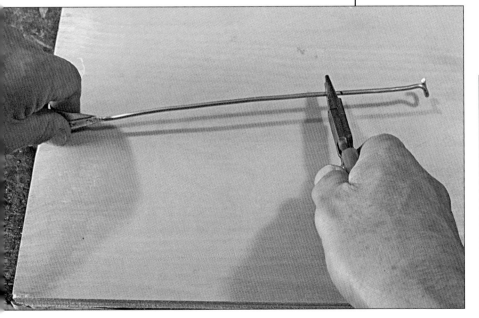

In this demonstration we are **adjusting the bend point and putting the pliers slightly on the long side of the mark**. Experience of which way you have had to correct by rolling the loop will inform this decision.

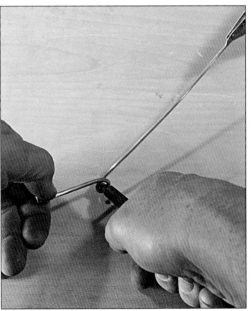

Second bend. The short end has then been lifted up and over the pliers to form the loop in the now straightened rod.

Final adjustment occurs just as with the linear elements connecting horizontals. Roll the loop toward the low side. Make small adjustments. If you used a right angle bent loop to connect the current element to the rest of the mobile, you can do fine adjustments on the balance by bending the right angle in or out, adjusting the length of that section a bit.

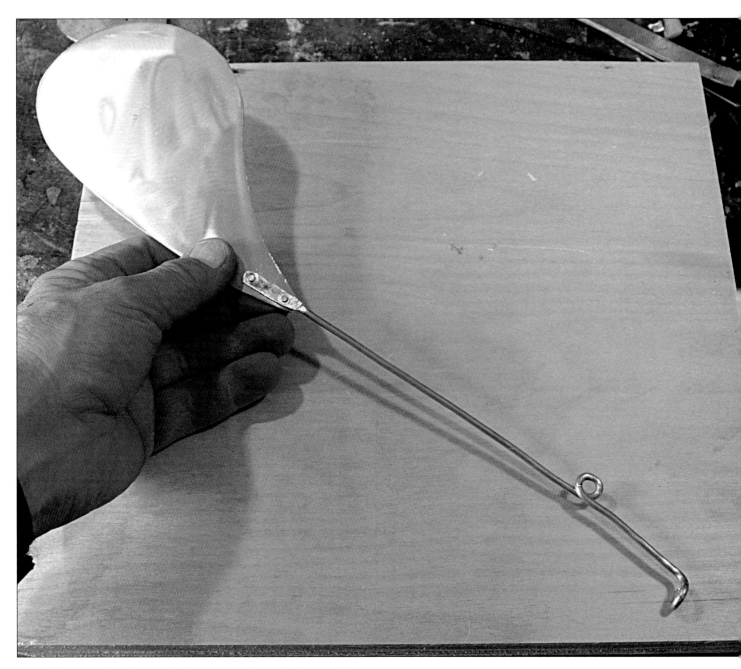

The completed vertical element ready to join the mobile.

Repeat if there are more vertical elements. There is nothing here that suggests that vertical elements must be above horizontal elements. It is just the way that this mobile example was accomplished.

Chapter 11

Rivet Removal and Other Repairs

The path to artistic satisfaction is rarely smooth. The drawing master throws out more than she saves. If the photographer realizes one bang-up image per roll of film or digital session, he is doing very well. What makes you, gentle reader, think that you are immune from the need to make serious adjustments?

One of the things that may happen is that a bail on a horizontal element got in the wrong place by some combination of errors, and the element is a shape that you really like, and you think you can save it by making the bail a little different shape. Or perhaps a vertical element wound up with a rod that was too short. You know the story, "I've cut it off three times and it's still too short!" That story. In any case, you need to remove the rivets and try again.

It is a fairly simple process. Center punch the rivet on the countersunk side, and then gently drill out the rivet body. This can be done without enlarging the hole, if you are very careful about exactly where you put the center punch mark.

Center punching the flat, countersunk side of the rivet. The squashed side of the rivet cannot be trusted to be centered on the hole, but this side can be.

If the punch mark is not in the center, then use the center punch to drift it toward the center. **Put the point in the mark**, lean the punch toward the center and punch again. This will make the hole a bit deeper, but move it in the direction the punch is pointed.

We have finally decided that the linear element is too short and no amount of cutting it off has helped the situation. We have to pull the rivets and attach a new linear element, hopefully long enough.

The ball of wax is very handy for lubricating the drill. Just **punch the drill in the wax before drilling the metal**. Using a drill *smaller* than the rivet diameter, **drill a pilot hole**.

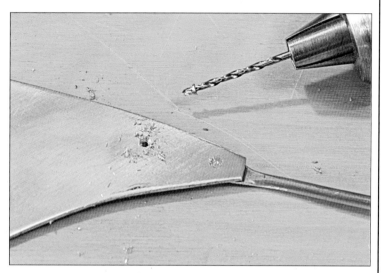

Using a drill *the size of the rivet*, **drill down the pilot hole**. With just a bit of working the drill at slight angles, the countersunk portion of the rivet should come out of the countersunk hole onto the drill. Success.

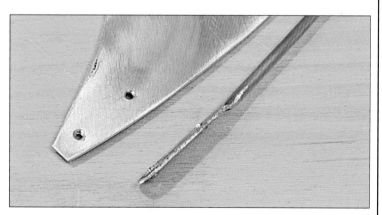

Both holes drilled out and the linear element removed. Ready for another.

Having demonstrated the rivet removal, we come to the place for the main warning. Over half the time it is actually easier to just start over cutting out a new piece of sheet metal and doing the filling, sanding, and buffing, than it is to try and save the old piece. Sometimes the repair is straightforward, but often there is enough wierdness with the element and its connections that starting over is easier. If there is only one thing that has to be done, and it is fairly obvious, go ahead and drill out the rivets and do the repair. More than one problem with an element should cause you to cut new metal and start over.

Other repairs.

Sometimes, after a number of corrections a linear element gets some wrinkles in it. We would like a way of straightening the rod, without having to start over. If it is too far gone, cut a new rod. But little wrinkles and bends can be tapped out. Roll the bar on the anvil plate and gently tap down on the high spots.

Straightening a bent linear element by tapping down the high spots. Go around a few times, tapping gently.

Then there is the misshapen center loop. If the pliers slip just a tiny bit, or you have rolled it back and forth a couple of times to achieve balance, the loop can get out of round. There are a couple of ways to save it. In the case that is is just a bit long, place it in the vise and give it a gentle squeeze.

A loop with an open bottom positioned in the vise for closure.

A misshapen loop mounted in the vise, with the legs of the linear element snug along the side of the vise jaws.

As the jaws **squeeze the loop to nearly circular**, the legs riding the vise jaws stay straight.

In the case of a wrinkle at the bottom, the best way to straighten that is to roll the wrinkled part up on the loop and then bring it back to straight with some wide pliers.

If the loop is open on the bottom, back to the vise jaws.

The loop has been shut. **Give the vise a little extra squeeze to prevent any spring back.**

Chapter 12

Hanging and Swivels

The whole point of the mobile building is to fill a section of the overhead with shape, color, and movement. So we need to get our creation in the air, and be confident that it will at once continue to move, and at the same time stay centered where we put it.

A super light weight mobile constructed with the chapter two technique can be secured with a piece of thread and a push pin.

A larger mobile from the later chapters needs a bit firmer hold on the overhead than a push pin in the acoustic tile. A thin string or fish line, knotted around a nail or the screw head on a vent grate will do nicely.

The thread for the very light weight mobile and the string for the more substantial work share the charac-teristic of torque. As the mobile turns in the breeze, the thread twists. The thread or string only wants to twist so far. Then the torque developed on the string will balance the torque from the breeze. Then the mobile will stop turning, and with the slightest change in the breeze, turn back in the other direction. Often, this is a nice movement. If the air currents working the mobile are consistent, always coming from the same direction with the same intensity, what can happen is that the string winds up and then the mobile just stalls at one point, no longer moving. The fix in that kind of environment is the swivel. Deep sea fishermen use a particularly nice ball bearing swivel. Putting one of these on the mobile will ensure continued movement.

Ball bearing swivels from the fishing store: a large one, usually only for the largest mobiles; a tiny one, good for most aluminum mobiles under 2 meters in diameter; and a package of medium sized swivels. Also there is a tiny split ring that we will use to hang the mobile.

The trick with these little jewels is getting the snap hook off and replacing it with a better looking jump ring. As with much else described here, there are many ways you could get your swivel attached, this is just one way. It might be a good way to start as you branch out and make mobile technique your own.

In short, clip off the snap hook, open a tiny split ring, and put it through the hole left by the hook wire, and then thread the mobile rod through the jump ring.

Open the split ring with a knife blade, enough to drop the swivel's now open little hole onto the now exposed leg of the split ring.

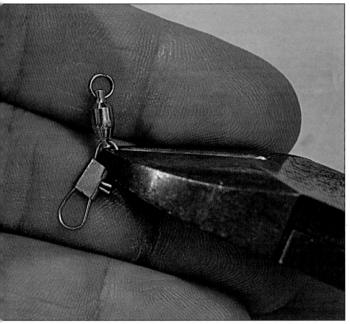

Cut the snap clip off with diagonal cutters.

Push the swivel around the split ring until it comes to the little crossover point. It will lock and stay there.

With the snap clip off, **see a tiny hole left where the clip was attached.** It doesn't look like the split ring will get in there, but it will be close enough.

Before attaching the top element to the rest of the mobile, **run the split ring through the end loop of the element up to the center loop. Then attach your string** to the ceiling.

Or you might put the swivel at the top of the string and not worry about the look of the hook.

Another use for the swivel is for a section of mobile that you want to move independently of another section. A swivel between those sections instead of the loop joint will allow free swinging of everything below the swivel.

What knot? So if you thought there were a lot of ways to design and build a mobile, take a look at how many knots you could use. Between your boy scout knots, sailor knots, fisherman knots, surgeon knots, the world of knitting and crocheting, and even truckers' knots, there are unnumbered varieties. Here we presume to present only one knot, sometimes called the half blood knot, the uni-knot, or fisherman's knot, it is used to attach fish line to a hook or swivel. Leave some extra length and start it loose.

Start the *half blood knot* by **taking two wraps around the ring**. Keep it all loose when wrapping this knot and leave a long tail.

Then **twist the working part of the string around the standing part five or six times**. Shown here, with the big rope, are four wraps. A couple more would be useful in fishing line, thread, or string.

Then **poke the working part of the string through the two loops**.

Now **poke the working part of the line through the loop** formed when you went from the end of the twist down to the two loops.

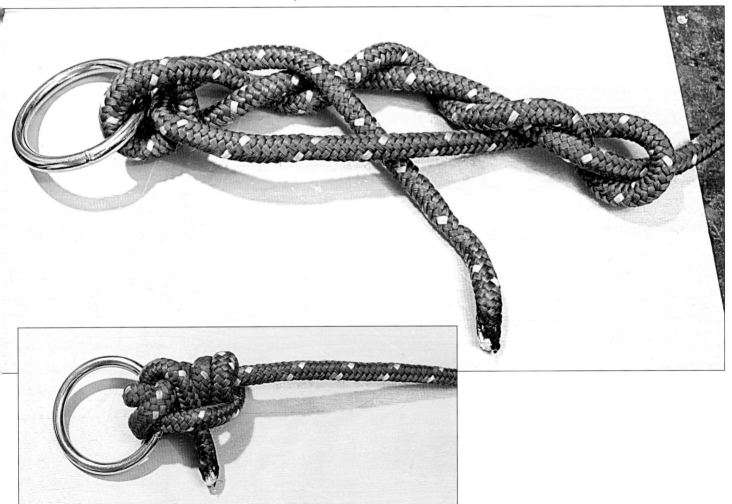

Now **pull it tight**, with both the standing part and the working part, **then cut off the working part close to the knot**. When jammed tight, the half blood knot can also be called a hatchet knot, because that's what you will have to use to untie it. It is pretty secure.

The half blood knot is a good knot attaching to the mobile. When installing the the mobile to the ceiling attachment it is important to keep the length of the standing part constant as you snug up the knot. Here are some modifications to the half blood for the top attachment. Use one loop through the attachment point, snug up the twists by passing the working part through the attachment point and pulling gently. Then finish off with one or two half hitches pulled tight.

Snug-up the knot by **pulling up down on the working part**. This should leave the standing part of the string the same length.

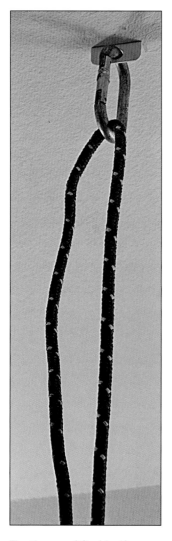

For the *modified half blood knot*, used to tie the mobile to the ceiling fixture, **put the string through the fitting only once.**

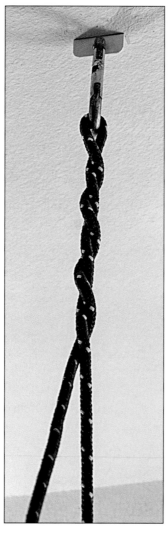

Then **make five or six twists around the standing part** with the working part of the string.

Next, **push the working part through the fixture again.**

Adjust the height of the mobile carefully before snugging this knot, as it is very hard to remove without cutting. Finish off the knot with **one or two half hitches and trim the working part.**

These two knots are pretty secure in string, thread, or fish line. If the line has been knotted top and bottom, and observations dictate a different height for the mobile, don't try to save the line. Cut it off and start over. A better way is to tie the half blood knot onto the mobile, then draw it up to the presumed best height with the line through the ceiling fixture and clamp it in place with a paper clip, hemostat, or spring clamp. Then take the ladder away and consult on the height with all concerned. If it takes a week to decide, so be it. When it is really good, then come back with the ladder, reclaim the clamp and do the top knot.

Getting it attached to the ceiling. By now, we know enough about riveting and bails that we can think of a way to make an attractive fitting for the ceiling. For most ceilings, if we can find a stud, a single screw into the stud through the drywall will hold up just about anything we are likely to be able to build. Then we just need some-thing that attaches to the screw and has a loop for the string. If you need to hang the mobile without a stud available, then hold it up with drywall anchors. Two anchors separated by a couple of centimeters (around an inch) will usually hold a good sized mobile. Then we need a little bigger fitting that attaches the screws to a loop or hole for the string.

While we are working, we need a way to hang up the mobiles without having to climb up on stools or ladders each time we add an element to a developing piece. One of the better ways is to fashion a rod with a hook in each end. Standing on the floor we can hook the bottom hook on the mobile and reach with the upper hook to the ceiling. After a bit, you may have a variety of lengths of hook rods for working the mobile in various states and a short one or two to store the mobile higher between creative sessions.

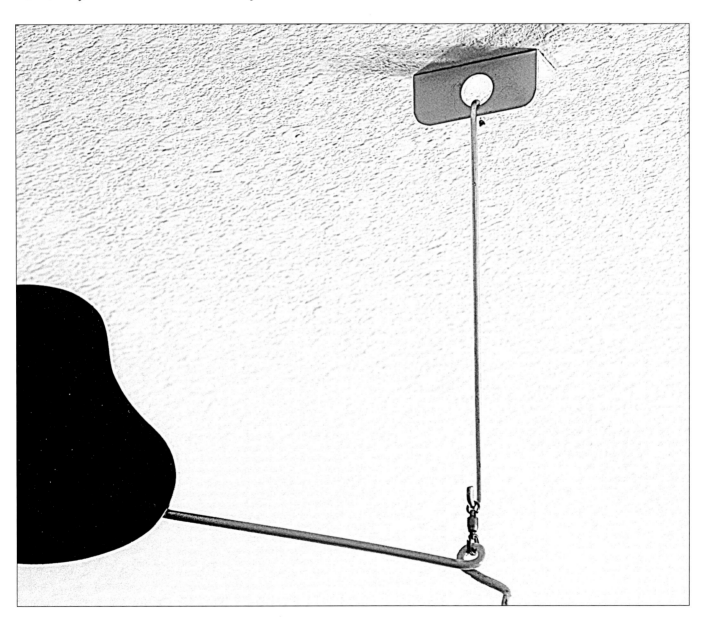

A temporary hanger made from a thin rod with a hook in each end.

Chapter 13

Finishing Considerations

The main obstacle to finishing is disassembly. We have the mobile nicely balanced and hanging up and moving in the breezes. Then we have to reduce it to a pile of elements and little tags for painting. There might be a fear that we will never get it back together again the same way. It's okay to have that sort of fear. We can recognize it, make friends with it, and overcome such fears to make the mobile even better. The key is organization. We are going to number or letter each of the pieces, and note that on our map, and we can return each element to where it was, bright and shiny with no mysteries or hassle.

We are going to make a system. It doesn't matter exactly what the system is, but the fact of a system will allow us to disassemble without fear. Well, maybe not without any fear, but with just a tiny bit of fear instead of mind numbing panic. What is described here is one system that has been found to work. Certainly others are possible, and almost no one who goes on to make multiple mobiles will wind up using the described system exactly as written. What is important is to use this system and your own experiences to organize your work in a that works best in your hands, mind, and studio.

The system described here is simple. Numbers for the horizontal and vertical elements, and letters for the linear elements. Any linear element riveted to a vertical element doesn't need to be tagged, it is now part of the vertical element. Only the separate linear elements need to be tagged.

What to tag with? Bits of tape, paper, or cardboard will get soggy from the paint, and quickly fall apart. We need to find some material that will not be disturbed by the paint, and lo, it is right at hand. Aluminum will do nicely, and we already have some in hand. How to mark the aluminum? Any kind of marker or grease pencil won't do, because we are going to paint it. Those marks will be covered quickly. What we can do is punch the numbers into the aluminum. The depressions will not fill up with paint like just scratches would, and can likely be seen from both sides of the tag. So here's the technique in a nutshell. Cut up little tags of thin aluminum. The thickness we used for the trial mobile way back in chapter two would be very nice. Drill a hole in one or both ends of each tag. Make a passel of jump rings. Mark each tag with a number or a letter. Then take the mobile

apart from the top down, and tag each element as it comes off the mobile according to its number on the map, using a jump ring to attach the tag to the element. Paint, then reassemble from the bottom up. Tweak and touchup, and the mobile is done!

Winding a coil of jump rings on a bar held in the vise. This is electric fence wire, in this case. Just about any bendable wire would work.

Cutting the coil into individual jump rings. Just chop them off. Make a few more than you think you might need.

Tags made from thin aluminum, with numbers and letters punched in with center punch dots. The letters will be clearly visible, even when repeatedly painted.

A tag attached to a linear element. This tag letter was made with a steel letter stamp. Number and letter stamps may be a luxurious extravagance but if you already have some, by all means, use them.

Now, we have decided to disassemble the mobile and paint the elements. What color to paint them? Some mobiles may be just right painted all one color. But here is an opportunity to introduce variety. If the mobile is going to hang in a known space, this might be an opportunity to look at the colors in the space and jump off of those colors for some of the mobile colors. One tactic for this jumping off is to detect a major pastel color in the space and to use a more saturated version of that hue to blend in a little, just as you are trying to attract attention. On the other hand, if the mobile is expected to be a major design statement in a space, the lucky patron to wind up with the mobile can redecorate the space to make it reflect the theme of the mobile.

Find what colors might look good together by copying the map and coloring in the elements with markers or crayons. A computer user of photo manipulation software can easily figure out how to do this given a scan of the map drawing, or even a digital photo of the mobile hanging unfinished. In any case, try your color combinations on paper or computer screen first. Try a bunch of different combinations, gradually converging on the best look for your creation.

Then, what kind of paint to use? There are all manner of compounds that can be made to stick to aluminum. From powder coating, being extremely durable, to a kindergarten tempera, there's a way to get the stuff to stick. Here, we will describe a way of finishing that results in a durable, colorful finish that can be had with little research or experimentation. Cans of brand name spray paint, properly applied on squeaky clean metal can be assured to make a long lasting even finish, but only if you use the same brand all the way through the process. So pick an easily accessible brand of paint that has a range of colors that will cover your likely selections. In recent years, some paint manufacturers have changed their chemistry. Some of this is for durability, some for environmental reasons, some because of companies merging or brand names being bought out. So, even if you have a couple of old cans of Pssst brand paint in the garage, and you are going to use Pssst brand on your mobile, buy all new cans of Pssst for the project. You really need the chemistry to be the same.

The spray can method is not the be all and end all of mobile finishing. It is one way to get color, durable and repeatable. The artist that wants an exact hue not sold in a can at the local paint emporium will want to expand on these possibilities. Acrylic or oil, sprayed or airbrushed over a sturdy primer can give spectacular results. More work, more experimentation, but it may well be worth it. For a first finished mobile, the spray can technique will get you started.

We did part of the preparation for painting when we sanded or buffed the elements, and sanded the linear element wires before bending. The next part of the preparation is cleaning. There are a few solvents that will do this job well, one of them is acetone. Use this stuff with extreme care. It is very volatile, poisonous and extremely flammable. This needs to be used in a well ventilated place and using an organic vapors respirator. Also use rubber gloves. Heavy ones or disposable latex, either kind. Wear goggles to prevent splashes of solvent in the eyes.

It's a bunch of work, to use the acetone and get all suited up with the protective gear, but when you've cleaned the mobile with this stuff it is really, really clean. Now, don't touch it again. Use latex gloves to prevent the slightest bit of finger oil from getting on our hard cleaned work. It is hard to believe how much cleanliness helps until you've messed up a few paint jobs. This is all written in hopes that you will have to mess up fewer jobs to learn this particular painful lesson.

Next we need a way to hang up the part to dry. Hanger wires do the job. Also you will need a place to hang the freshly painted elements where the air is still and no one will bother them or stir up dust around them. Since we are already good at bending wires, prepare some "S" hangers and some place to hang them and the suspended wet painted elements.

Lay out some paper. Then tape it down. This just keeps the paint from getting all over the bench. One would not think that would be a problem, except that when cleaning subsequent batches of elements, the acetone rag might well pick up some of that paint from the bench and then spread it on the elements you are trying to clean. The paper just allows us to bundle up the mess and throw it away all at once after painting.

When we actually spray the paint, we will want the element being painted elevated from the paper. If we set it on the paper and paint, then the paint at the edges of the element does not come out even.

Now we could be ready to paint. We have reduced fear with planning and organization, we have each element, linear, horizontal, and vertical extremely clean, we have a painting zone papered, and a landing zone for each element.

Chapter 14
Painting

With all the preparations done, it has come to setting aside the time to actually do the painting. You really cannot hurry this phase. There's the time in applying the paint, and then there is drying time. It going to take a few sessions, with many hours of drying time between to get a good finish on the mobile parts. Leave time for this part of the job. Don't be promising delivery a day after you have the bare aluminum mobile balanced and hanging up.

Start with the horizontal elements on their bottom sides. Put an S hook on the number tag's jump ring.

Grasp the bail with a gloved hand and lightly spray two light coats of the flat while primer.

Grasp the bail and hook, then paint the bottom lightly.

If the first coat doesn't quite cover the metal, you are just about right. Put on a second coat, very lightly, a few moments after the first, which should bring you close to full coverage. Every time you set the paint can down, first turn it upside down and spray a few seconds until only propellant comes out of the nozzle. To avoid trashing other objects in the painting space, it is best to paint the inside of your trash can.

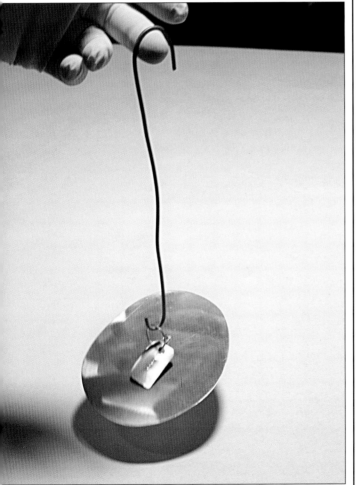

Hook the jump ring to make it easy to hang up the element for drying.

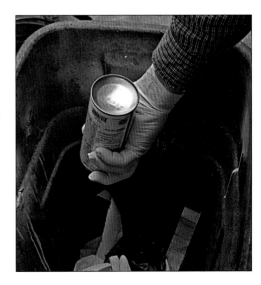

Clear the spray in the trash can.

That keeps down the accidental overspray problem. Hang the element up in your drying space and do the next element.

The linear elements can be laid out on the paper if desired and one side sprayed. Come at them from different angles with the spray to get paint on the insides of the loops. Now go away for a while. Give it a couple of hours before doing a second coat.

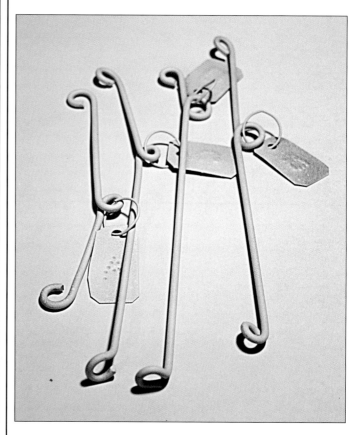

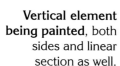

The first element hung up to dry.

Linear elements lined up to paint.

When the horizontal elements are done, start with the vertical elements. Hold one up by the S hook and do the two light coats on both sides. Hang it up to dry and repeat.

Look carefully at the first coat. If there is anywhere that the paint has run or formed a drip or thick place, you have found a place where the paint was put on too thick.

Vertical element being painted, both sides and linear section as well.

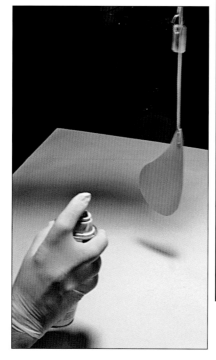

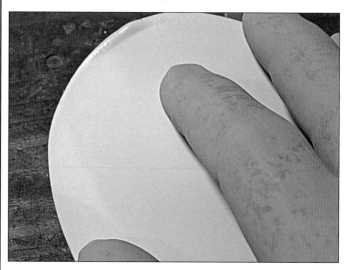

A paint run, at the top of the element. This one will have to be cleaned off and done over.

If it is just a little run, you might be able to get away with it and cover it. Likely not. Take that element, get out the acetone can and some paper towels and just clean it off to the bare metal and start over. Ouch. Really. Starting over is really the easy way.

The second coat of primer proceeds as the first. Light coats, hanging up for drying. The horizontal elements get a second coat on the bottom side, and after it dries, the process is repeated on the top side. Turn over the linear elements and give them their two sessions of two light coats on the back side. The way it goes, you wind up with one painting session with just a couple of elements to do. Thats okay. No one said everything had to come out at exactly the same time, like a well planned family banquet.

With everything primed, it is time to do the colors. Nothing here tells how many parts are to be done with how many different colors. What is important, is some more organization. Take the map, now numbered with the colors, and take all the elements to be painted one color, and hang them in one area of the drying space. Segregate the elements by color, making it clearly obvious which elements get each color. Double check this

with the map. The time to do these checks and organization is when the air is clear and the spray cans capped. Run through it again in your head, "Okay, elements one, six, and eight get the blue, here in the corner. Elements three, four, and eleven get the yellow, hanging from the ladder...." A strong organization at this point really helps. It is too easy to get confused during the hurly-burly of the actual painting, with the action, movement, remembering to clear the nozzle, and all the protective gear. So anticipate the mood of actual spraying to get the colors organized at a more contemplative time.

Up until this point, a little overspray of one element's priming on to another one was no big deal. Now it is. The drying area needs to be well away from the spraying area. One puff of blue on those yellow elements will have you starting over. Pick a color, take an element from the drying area, take it to the spray table, and do the two light coats. Take it back and hang it up. Get the next element. When done with that color, do a final nozzle clear, let the paint in the air settle as you shake the next can of color. Look at the can. Look at the map, look at the element you are about to paint. Be double sure this is the color for this group and then proceed.

The top side of a large horizontal element being painted.

Sometimes it occurs that the vertical element wants to have a color while the linear element riveted to it wants to be left white or have a different color. Up until now, it seemed that the horizontal elements were harder to do because we were doing the tops and bottoms separately to keep the edges from getting paint build up. But now the vertical elements will become more of a project. To keep the color off the linear element, we need to mask it. Some fresh masking tape and paper, covering the entire linear element work well here. Raise the vertical element off the paper with a little block of wood and do a couple of light coats.

Let it dry there, and then do one or two more light coats to finish it off before moving it or turning it over. When there are a number of vertical elements to be done in this manner, it changes the organization a bit. Do the set up and masking when the paint is dry. Keep colors as far away from each other as possible, maybe even erecting cardboard barriers between them to keep the colors separate. Then suit up and spray. Try not to have to do much organizational thinking while spraying paint.

So tell me again why I can't just spray paint the mobile while it was hanging there, all balanced and put to-gether? It would seem like that could be done, especially if you wanted it to be all one color. But paint, in order to stick to the thing being painted is actually a form of glue. If we were to spray paint on the hung mobile, the paint would lodge in joints of the bails and loops and stick them together quite firmly. Even after we broke them loose, there would still be little cradles of paint to lock the mobile into one overall shape. Part of the delight of the mobile is its shape changing movement. It is the whole feeling of "mobileness" that we are keeping by separating the elements for painting.

Variations in painting practice are possible. There are some with airbrushed subtle color changes across the elements, there are some with abstract oil or acrylic designs brushed directly upon the elements. Large outdoor mobiles have been finished by powder coating, an industrial process of extreme durability. There's gold leaf or antique crackle finish. What has been described above is not the end and only way to finish the mobile. What has been described is a good way to get started, and for some of the other finishing processes a way to get a nice toothy primer of flat white.

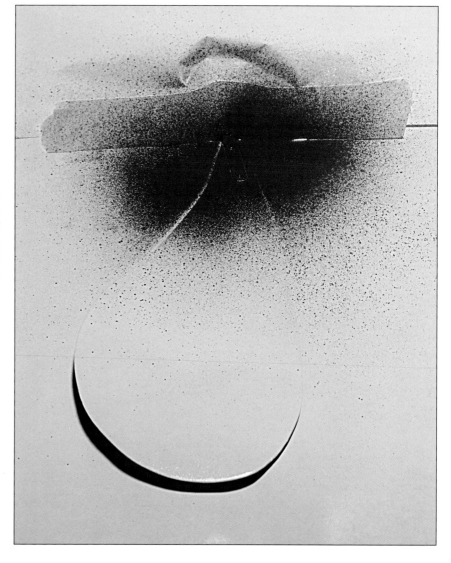

Vertical element with its linear element masked off. In this case we will be putting color on the portion of the linear element that is riveted to the vertical element. Note how the vertical element is raised up from the paper.

Chapter 15

Reassembly and Final Tweaks

Now we have a stack of painted mobile parts, perhaps in bright colors. Using the map, rebuild the mobile from the bottom up. This is the time for final tweaking and some touchup painting. As elements go back on the mobile, sometimes a linear element's orientation is not obvious. The map helps a bit, but if we have the correct element per the map and we can't figure out which end goes to which element or group, try one.

There's only two choices at this point and it is easy enough to switch when one group of elements bobs way down from where it was planned to float. Half the time you won't have to switch. As we work up the mobile, and the parts balance, it is time to close the loops. To avoid marring the hard earned paint job, pad the plier jaws that you are going to use to close those loops.

A pair of channel lock pliers padded with leather. Wet leather strips were stretched around the jaws and tied, then left to dry. They are on there very tight.

Another pair of **channel lock pliers padded with several layers of masking tape**.

Parallel jaw pliers padded with masking tape.

If you have left the loops open by just not closing
them all the way, it's the squeeze play that does the job.

Using the padded
channel locks to **close a
loop around the bail of
a horizontal element**.

If you have left the loops open with a twist, then the
two plier technique will bring them back together.

On a loop that was left
open by misaligning the
end of the loop and the
long section of the linear
element, **grasp the
shank of the element**
with one set of pliers,
and then **bend the loop
end into alignment**,
closing the opening in
the loop.

As we close the loops, sometimes this changes the balance slightly. Also the addition of the weight of the paint may have changed the balance slightly. We can make minor tweaks to the balance by adjusting the angle of end loops. Loops that are at a right angle to the rest of the linear element are the easiest to adjust. On the end that is low, change the angle inward. This will shorten the distance between the center loop and the end and allow that end to rise. If the right angle loop is on the high side, bend it outward to make that section longer and bring that end down. Even loops that are in line with the rest of the element can be lengthened or shortened

a little bit. If you do these tweaks as you reassemble the mobile you can make it nice and even.

Another thing that occurs is that vertical elements wind up not hanging perfectly vertical. They need a little twist. Grab the central loop of its linear element with padded pliers and hold it straight up and down. Then twist the vertical element back to vertical and a little bit to the other side. It should spring back close to vertical. Then let go of the loop and see how it hangs. Often this takes a couple of cycles of grab-twist-release-observe until the element is hanging just right.

Straightening a vertical element on a large mobile section.

Touching-up the bail of a horizontal element with the paint-soaked cotton swab.

Inspite of all of our care, some paint has been chipped, dinged, or marred. Not to worry; it can be touched up. We need to gather some cotton tipped swabs from the medicine cabinet and our spray paint. In a separate well ventilated area, such as outdoors, spray paint into the cap of the spray paint can for a few seconds, until a little pool of paint appears. Then go inside to the mobile and dab the paint on the affected section with the swab. This keeps us from stinking up the studio area for just a patch of paint, but gets the paint right where its needed. When the cotton tip becomes stringy, just use another one.

If some element was seriously marred, bad news. The easy way is to strip it down to the bare metal with acetone, and then do the whole paint job again. It's not often at this stage you will have to do that, but it's not unheard of. So if the retouch just can't cover the scale of the damage, that's your sign to wipe down and paint again. You may get to the point of not cleaning up the painting area until the mobile is hanging pretty.

Chapter 16

Packing and Hanging

Now if we were doing jewelry, we could just pop the work between two layers of cotton, tape some bubble wrap about it, and ship it off with perfect confidence. The mobile artist has a different problem. The materials we use are pretty sturdy, but as we have created some extent, some long distances with them, they are subject to being bent in transit, or even in packing unless we approach the task with care.

As with the whole business of taking the mobile apart, painting it, and then reassembling it, this packing and shipping business need not generate fear, just good planning and caution.

The best way to ship, store, or even deliver around the corner, is to lay the mobile out flat and keep it that way until the instant they are to float in their display space. Many mobiles will lay flat. these are the easiest to ship. If they won't lie flat in one piece, then it may be that divided into two or three pieces, the pieces will lay flat. The main objective here is to keep the linear elements from being bent and to keep elements from touching one another during transit.

This can be done with holes and string.

Part of a large **mobile tied to a thin plywood door** skin with string strung through holes drilled in the plywood.

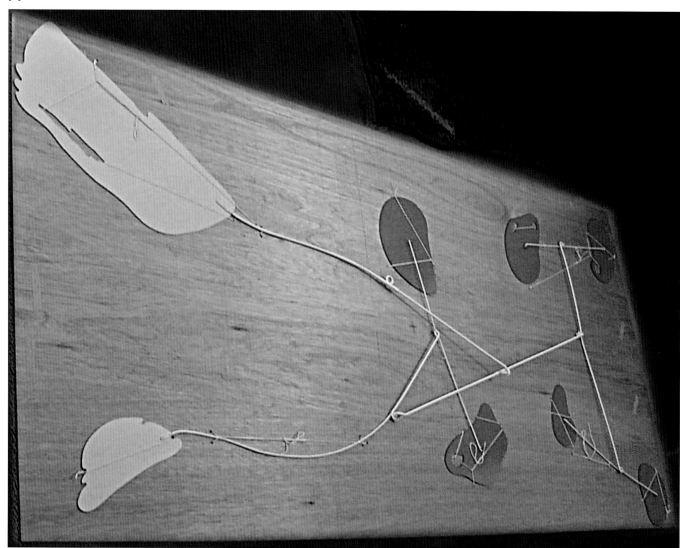

Or it can be done with tape and cardboard.

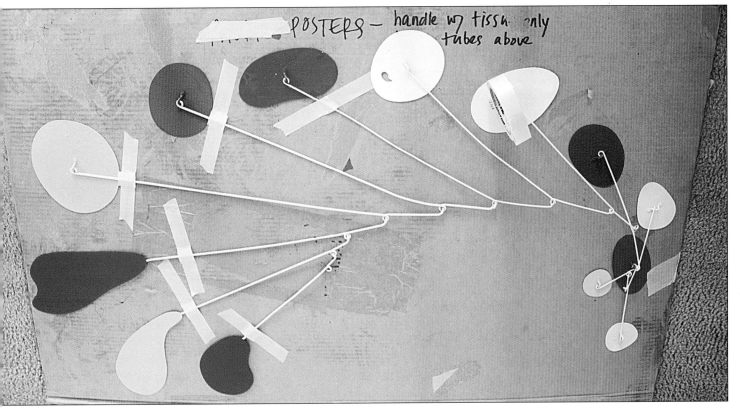

A smaller **mobile taped to a piece of cardboard** for temporary storage or local transportation.

Also possible are wood and glued velcro, gluing hook side velcro to the mounting board and then using strips of loop side velcro to bridge the linear elements.

To be real helpful to the person repacking the mobile (even yourself after some time) put drawing of the mobile on the mounting board, with each colored element outlined in its color.

Boxes of many sorts can be purchased or constructed. For small mobiles, there are some flat boxes sold for protecting paintings. Some of these can be sized to the mounting board. The gold standard is the wooden box. Anyone with a background in woodworking, be it high school shop up to professional cabinet makers, can construct flat box of narrow lumber ends and edges with thin plywood sides. While it is true that most of your shipping costs are for the protective box rather than the art work, it is worth it to insure that the work arrives intact and hangs the way you had last seen it in your studio.

[diversionary story] Some time ago, I was exhibiting some electro-kinetic sculptures in a show with a neon artist. I arrived with the sculptures in sturdy boxes made to fit and cradle each piece. Once I had unscrewed the lids of the boxes, plugged in the sculptures to check operation and was removing and mounting one of the works on the wall, the neon artist came over, looked over my whole setup and said, "Wow, those are really nice boxes!" Having spent considerably more time on the works than the rough wood boxes, I was a bit put out. I found out a few minutes later that the neon artist had taken the works from the studio wall, several hundred miles away, laid them carefully down in the bed of a rented van and driven to the gallery. This artist and the gallery curator had just spent the last three days bending new tubes for all of the neon pieces in the show. [end diversion]

Another nice touch with the box, especially if there is a gallery involved that will store the box, is to take a photograph of the piece in the studio before packing and glue it to the outside of the box. Gallery folk do earn their cut, but asking them to relate the active gossamer piece hanging from their ceiling to a particular bit of packing gathering dust in the back room is a bit much. That little photo on the box will do wonders at that sensitive time when they are jazzed by just having sold your mobile, to get it properly packed so the buyer actually gets a piece that looks like the thing that hung in the gallery.

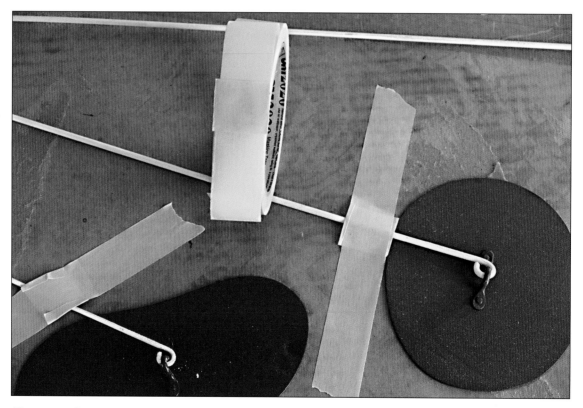

Close-up of the masking tape technique. To keep the tape from sticking to our carefully completed paint job, a small piece of the tape is reversed and stuck to the sticky side of the large piece crosswise. This is the section that bears on the painted linear element.

Chapter 17

Expanding on Basic Designs

A wave crashes on the rocks, a new theory of quantum gravity is explained, a drop of blood splatters on the kitchen floor. Any one might be a mobile. A sweeping upward gesture of the arm may lead to the whole feeling of a mobile to fill a high ceilinged entryway. So, how do you get from the idea to the design for a mobile? How do you get from that vague feeling that there is a good concept here, to a plan for cutting metal? It's not enough to say, "It just came to me." That doesn't teach creativity. Creativity is a skill of mind that can be learned, and a habit, that if cultured for some time will provide artistic riches.

You learned how to use the pliers and the tinsnips, now learn how to use the mind. As tools are different, so are minds. These are general guidelines and a plan to get a few ideas from concept to mobile. Your mind works differently than anyone else's. But we are all more the same than we are different. We share a common structure, in hand and eye, as well as the structure of the brain. All of our experiences make us different, but we start from a common working structure.

What follows serves to get the subconscious part of that common mind structure to be working for us, not against us. We need techniques to activate these basic structures of the mind that we all have in common. These are tricks to get that to happen. We'll do two things. First we will put the idea into the mind in as many different ways as possible, then we will activate the subconscious to work on what we stuffed in there.

Let's do this in a step by step fashion from an initial idea to the plan for an actual hanging mobile. The actual order of the steps may not actually be important, but there is a progression.

Step One The big idea. Write down the idea. (oh hey, new theory of quantum gravity, I could do a mobile on that.)

Step Two Sketch what the idea seems to be, diagram the idea, (okay, this quantum gravity thing is related to string theory — I can use that, the strings look like this.)

Step Three Paint the idea. (here's the strings in red and the particles of quantum gravity in blue, and the membrane of space-time in the pinkish grey) Look at the painting and then look at the rag you used to wipe the brushes. (ooo, look at the blue smear across the patch of pinkish grey!)

Step Four Cut out little bits of colored paper and move them around the table or sketch pad. Tape them to a piece of paper when they have suggested something. (there's the pinkish grey patch, and this looks like the blue smear, but where are the strings?)

Step Five Sketch the idea again, sketch or use a copier to make a mirror image of the idea. Transparency sheets are great, copy it onto a trans sheet and then flip the sheet over and copy that. Reduce, enlarge, combine and copy, whatever the copier will do. Cut the mirror image pieces and tape them back together (here's the smear and patch done three times in a triangular three fold path, and the strings appear to hold them all together)

Step Six Write a little song, ditty, or poem about the idea or the idea and its mirror image. Sing or read the ditty, perform it.(strings to the right of me, membranes to the left, here am I, stuck in the middle with time, pink and blue, pink and blue, pink and blue...)

Do you feel silly yet? (yes, about half past step four, but I want this idea, so I'll go on)

Step Seven Cut out one little piece of sheet metal in a shape related to or derived from the idea or the idea's derivatives (well, the blue smear sort of looked like this)— hold it up to the light, look at it's shadow, fold it, fold it back to flat and pound it flat, then fold it a different way. Fold it back to flat again. Put it down on a piece of paper and run a pencil around the outline. Flip it over and do it again. Make a bunch of those outlines in a circle. Maybe do another piece of sheet metal, maybe not.

Step eight, bend some wire. Take the pliers and a length of wire and while looking at what had gone before, bend wire in a three dimensional shape that might or might not tie some of the artifacts previously created together. Maybe even fashion little places in the wire matrix for bits of the colored paper or metal cutouts to reside.

Step nine, now lay all of this stuff out before you. (egad! what a bunch of trash. I hope nobody else sees this) Quietly sip your favorite beverage and don't ask anything of yourself. Push one thing around, uncover another. Don't try to think of anything, just very quietly play around.

No more steps. Somewhere in there, there is an idea that will come knocking in that quiet time. Somewhere down in that gray matter in your skull is idea that will come tapping on the door of working memory saying, "Hey boss, are you interested in me?" The process of being quiet and just pushing stuff around for a while is actually the process of opening the door of working memory and providing an empty chair at the table for that lonely thought to sit down and chat for a while. That first idea that came in might not be the one that will make the perfect mobile out of your initial idea, but be nice to it. You want it to go back and tell its friends that the door is open and they might want to surface for a while.

The first time you try this, it feels like utter futility. "What am I doing here, staring at this pile of paper and junk?", you might cry. Okay. Put the stuff away. At night, when you are dropping off to sleep, gently remind yourself that you are actually looking for an idea, and it would be real nice to come up with something in the next few days. Write yourself a note, that you will see as you climb into the sack, about the idea. Or put the envelope of stuff you were looking at near the bed or under the pillow just to key yourself to use the magic drowsy time to get in touch with the rest of your mind that is churning about when you are dropping off to sleep. Just keep mentioning as you go to sleep how nice an idea would be.

A few days later, at a quiet moment, pull the stuff from the idea development phase out again and spread it out and mess about with it. Ask yourself, "Is there anything here that could hang from the ceiling? Anything at all?" Be quiet for a while. Let something come knocking on working memory. For some folk, it may work the first time. For others the idea may come at a totally inappropriate time, but just a little doodle will be enough to capture it. Even if the doodle is done with ball point on your palm because the idea came in the middle of a hugely important business meeting. And for still others, still no transition from idea to mobile plan will bubble up. Not everyone makes this happen the first time.

"Now this has gone far enough", you say. It may be that you have gone through all the falderal described and still no flash of "inspiration". Time to cut out some sheet metal. Take out a small sheet and lay out some shapes. Cut out a few and push them around the workbench. Your idea may not actually be in the shapes, your idea might be in the spaces between the shapes on the bench.

It may occur that the flash of inspiration did not come, at least not on the idea you initially wrote down. But look now at the shapes that you have cut out. Do they look like the ones in the last mobile? Likely not. In the case that they are not the same as the last mobile, make a mobile out of that particular relationship of shapes. That big flash idea may have to wait for later and you can just settle for a gentle evolution of style.

Let's just say that the idea did turn into a plan for a mobile. What do we do now? Sketch it out, cut metal. Try to make the mobile work in a sketch. Then cut metal for the elements. Make a sample with as few pieces as will support and demonstrate the basic plan. See if it works hung from the ceiling. Often times the sketch phase of development will show up a flaw in the concept or plan. Or it might be that it looked good on the sketch, but when you cut and hang sheet metal and rods, You just can't seem to make it work.

But you can ask, "How many elements will this idea/plan actually support, could there be too many? Could there be too few?" These and other questions and answers rushing about the mind may be the key to getting that plan into mobile form.

Sketch again, make a plan with numbers and letters and thoughts about how large the largest element will be and how small the smallest. Now cut metal for the real mobile.

Very often, doing the above path, you will be on your way to something delightful and a new direction and expanded vision of mobiles. (wait, wait, what happened to the quantum gravity idea?)

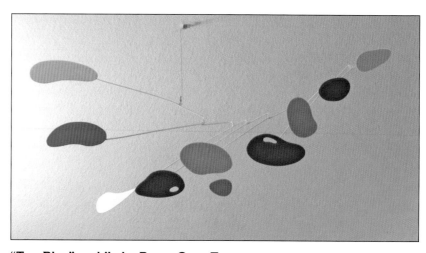

"Two Blue" mobile by Bruce Cana Fox

Chapter 18

Developing a Personal Style of Mobiles

Developing a personal style is a bit more serious than just expanding on your basic design. At this point we have made "some" mobiles and have "prospects" for making more. That's about the time the "personal style" issue comes up. People talk about it for marketing or it may occur that you, the artist yourself, are unsatisfied and searching for something.

It is probably a poor idea to go looking for a personal style before one has gained control of the medium. While there is no minimum number of mobiles to have created before declaring control of the medium, the level of frustration with the tools and the path of creation should have settled down to very seldom.

The fact of doing mobiles at all is a personal style. The whole community of mobile makers is not very big. How many people do you know who come into an art gallery and look up at all, ever? So if you can do a nice mobile, you may be already there, as far as a personal style is concerned. If you wind up nearly copying or springing off of other folks' mobiles for the first little while, thats not a problem.

Sooner or later you may want a personal style of mobiles. Something that a person in the know about mobiles can look up and say, "I know that person, that's (insert your artistic handle here)! You can want that, but rarely can you consciously go out and achieve it. If you look back at the works you have done, there may actually be a common thread in them. (You did take pictures of the ones that left the studio, didn't you?) What comes, is that with experience and production you do more and more of what you like and in ways you like. When it's, "I'm doing a series on the recent quantum theory of gravity" in your mobiles, likely there is a personal style there. And it could wind up quite distinctive.

But for the sake of argument, let's just assume there isn't the common thread, and you feel that the work is "all over the map", and what is really called for is the full court press for that personal style.

Oh, you could be the one with the lacy edges on all the elements. Or the one with the really big hole in the elements, or the one that makes mobiles that each look like an octopus crawling about upside down on the ceiling. Or the one whose linear elements are all welded into truss shapes. Or the one with the hundred different shades of blue kidney bean shapes. Or the one with the

little blown glass counterweights. Dueling rhinoceroses thunder above a shark infested veldt. Go fish, go figure. But, remember, you are going to have to like the work to keep up the production. It's hard enough doing art, without trying to do art that you don't like or in a process you can't stand anymore. So what the style should become is more what you like to do rather than a marketing stratagem.

To get there, what we need to search for is more joy. We need to test a pack of different ways to a mobile and measure the joy in that mobile and the process that built it. We need to take each measurement and bounce it off the things that we did before, and ask, "Was that better?" Do I feel better about the time I spent and the mobile result than I was feeling on the last mobile? Better than the first mobile I made? Each little positive increment in joy helps us turn in the right direction. And it should be abundantly clear when something is productive of less joy.

One way to create these variations is restriction. Too much freedom and we roam all over the place. An artificial limit, self imposed usually, may well spur creativity as we improve within the new boundaries. So, only two colors? No paint at all? Only one element painted? No more kidney shapes? Every element must have one right angle? No right angle loops? No straight lines? No deep curves on any linear element? No vertical elements? No horizontal elements? Just linear elements? Any sort of restriction like that will start you in some other direction. But which one is right?

Just as with finding music we like, finding a mobile style involves trying different stuff. With music we can tune around the radio dial, listening to twenty different tunes in not much more time than it takes to tell about it. We've heard much stuff we don't like in that time, and then settled on a station that is playing stuff we connect with. It takes a little longer with building mobiles. You may experience false starts, such as a whole style of mobile that just isn't making it for you and you wind up just scrapping the mobile rather than go on to finish something you don't actually like. There may have been other styles you were able to complete, and you may have hung, sold, given away, or put in a box in the loft, but when completed didn't look bad at all. But if that style didn't result in more joy of building and displaying it is a dead end. Better to find that out sooner. But it is important to try many different kinds of shapes and construction methods to arrive at the process and results that connect with you.

Back when we were starting to build mobiles, there were different things done, along the path of getting control of the medium. Some looked better than others. And now we do different things to be on the path of seeking more joy in building to look for distinctive personal style of mobile.

You may restrict this and then that, making a mobile or two in each emerging style, and determine each time that what was restricted from the style was not the right choice. Some restrictions may not be by choice. Just the size of the space you have to work in might keep your work necessarily small. But the style search may take a while and you should delight in all the discoveries along the path. The sketches may be enough, because after a few mobiles and their sketches, your ability to sketch something that can be build and balanced has improved. On the path of restriction, you may well find a style to nurture your muse for some time.

Another way get at the style is to expand the palette. Look around and ask yourself, what of that lathe and milling machine? Can I do work on those that would hang and balance well? I could have someone sand cast bronze fittings that tie the elements together? Look at this lanyard from the war surplus junk store, look at these huge rivets, look at the bale of funky looking bent pieces of metal, and so on. "Oh, if I carved this long stick as the central linear element, the mobile would look dramatic." "If I put a swivel at each joint the mobile wouldn't be so predictable." If you incorporate or reflect found things in the work, it may lead to another style.

Constrict the palette, expand the palette. Two ways to help evolve a personal style. Another thing we might do is to turn things. Take something we are doing and turn it around backwards, or upside down. Turn the color scheme, perhaps by taking the colors in turn and shifting each on by one or two colors of the rainbow. If we had been sketching mobiles from the bottom element first, up to the top, that's a candidate for a turn or reversal. If we had been doing the shapes first and then coloring in the shapes, perhaps to lay down colors and then draw shapes in those colors would be enough of a turn to result in a personal style. We were turning the linear element ends with pliers. We could turn that and make the loops by hand forging the rod ends; difficult, but possible, and distinctive.

The above experimentations were just to get us to do so many different things with the mobiles and expand the variety of methods of work and visual results. Hopefully, we couldn't help but find a process that made time melt away and a mobile result that gave us the big YESSSS! feeling. Forcing all of the variations gets us up and out of one rut, but hopefully not into another. A personal style does not mean that we cannot progress. A personal style based on our heartfelt joy at process and result is one that will carry the artist through many works, but will allow change. That change may be in pursuit of more joy at process and result.

In summary: try many things. Read omnivorously and voraciously Really get in touch with the processes you enjoy and the results that make you go YESSSS! Think about just what it was in that mobile that made you shout with joy to see it. Pick that one, refine it for more YESSSS! moments, and let it evolve. Don't let it become a rut, because the best personal style is the one that bring us the most joy. It will show in the work and those observing the work will be able to share that joy.

"Two Red" mobile by Bruce Cana Fox

Chapter 19
Sources of Tools and Materials

A tool store that had been a mainstay for twenty years just disappeared. It had only been a couple of months since the last visit, but last Thursday, gone. Empty storefront; phone number disconnected. It is a dynamic thing, this tool business. Sources of really nice stuff dry up and blow away even as other sources are found. What might be listed here, by the time other eyes see it, may just be a historical note. But it is a guide. In the world of the early twenty-first century, any thing being made can be found and usually quickly.

About the only oddball tool that you need to do mobiles is the pair of round nose pliers. MSC, currently at mscdirect.com has the tools and sells them over the internet, by phone, or catalog. They have also been found in small sizes at bead and jewelry supply stores. Some larger round nose pliers are available from blacksmith supply companies. There might only be a few of those in a country or region, so a search and mail/internet orders are the rule.

Kayne and Son sell blacksmith tools over the net and can be found at: Blacksmithdepot.com

They are located at: Kayne and Son Custom Hardware Inc. 100 Daniel Ridge Road, Candler, NC 28751. Tel: 88-667-8868.

The next hardest to find item in mobiles is the rivets. As long as they last, Hanson Rivet & Supply Co. is very good. They will ship to an individual with an address and a credit card. They are located at 13241 Weidner Street, Pacoima, CA 91331. Tel: 818-485-0500, and at www.hansonrivet.com.

I recommend their MS20426AD-3-3 rivets for large work and for smaller mobiles, their 78 CTSK 1/16x3/16. Contact them for a catalog and be prepared to be amazed at the variety of rivets available.

Sheet aluminum is available at metal supply stores. In the San Fernando Valley area of Los Angeles, Industrial Metal Supply is clearly superior. I can't recommend mail ordering sheet metal, although there must be a way.

This is one thing you need to go and feel and handle and carry away. Phone books and internet searches will find you the closest source. Until then, aluminum flashing can be found in the big home improvement stores.

Wire is a matter for search and collection. In the hardware store, when you see a wire that looks and feels like it would work for mobiles, buy it. If it works, go back and buy more. This wire selection business is another matter for feel and doesn't respond very well to mail order.

The rods for large mobiles can be found at the same sorts of places as the sheet metal. Ask around for rod in the sizes you are interested in. They might not be out in front like the sheet metal cutoffs. Aluminum welding rods can be found at welding supply stores. Once again, these may not be out on the sales floor but will have to be requested. When the kind counter man brings some out, look at it and make sure it is actually round and doesn't have a manufacturer's stamp every few centimeters. When that happens, asking if there are any other alloys available might get you a look at a different rod. When you look for welding supplies, another path is to look for Gas-Industrial. The folks who use the welding rods also use cylinders of Helium and Argon. So those suppliers will also carry some very nice sticks of aluminum.

The hallmark of finding mobile making materials is an outgoing, searching attitude. Be nice. Not everyone carries what you need, but you never know when someone who doesn't have what you need today might have something in the back room that you would need later. The key is to turn on your contacts' memory and searching attitude to pull up what might help you. If someone doesn't have what you want to do your mobiles, ask if they know someone who might carry such stuff. If you ask around, you will find what you need. The stuff to do mobiles of whatever size and style you want to make is out there.

Recommended Reading

The winner and still champion of metalworking books is:

Untracht, Oppi. *Metal Techniques for Craftsmen,* New York: Doubleday, 1968.

Other helpful books include:

Barnwell, George W. *The New Encyclopedia of Machine Shop Practice,* New York: Wm. H. Wise & Co., Inc, 1941.

Birdsall, G. W. *Do It Yourself With Aluminum*, New York: McGraw-Hill, 1955.

Meilach, Dona. *Direct Metal Sculpture, Revised and Expanded 2nd Edition,* Atglen, Pennsylvania: Schiffer Publishing, 2001.

Pirsig, Robert M., *Zen and the Art of Motorcycle Maintenance,* New York: William Morrow Publishers, 1974.

Untracht, Oppi. *Jewelry, Concepts and Technology*, New York: Doubleday, 1982.

"Sphere One" mobile by Bruce Cana Fox